THE ELUSIVE SELF

THE ELUSIVE SELF

based on
THE GIFFORD LECTURES
delivered in
THE UNIVERSITY OF EDINBURGH
1966-68

HYWEL D. LEWIS

THE WESTMINSTER PRESS
PHILADELPHIA

PUBLISHED BY THE WESTMINSTER PRESS®
Philadelphia, Pennsylvania

Typeset and printed in Hong Kong
9 8 7 6 5 4 3 2 1

Library of Congress Cataloging in Publication Data

Lewis, Hywel David.
  The elusive self.

  Includes bibliographical references and index.
  1. Self (Philosophy)—Addresses, essays,
lectures. 2. Dualism—Addresses, essays, lectures.
I. Title
BD450.L473   126   81-14691
ISBN 0-664-24404-1   AACR2

Contents

Preface

This book is the sequel, or perhaps I should say, a supplement, to my earlier book, *The Elusive Mind*. I had hoped, in one further volume, based more on the Second Series of my Gifford Lectures, to bring out more fully the implications for morality and religion of the views set forth in *The Elusive Mind* and in two interim books, *The Self and Immortality* and *Persons and Life after Death*. But the further things I wished to say about persons and their identity, as well as comment on more recent philosophical work on self-identity, set this further work so much apart from the remainder as to take its place better as a separate book on this theme alone.

The centrality of the question of the nature of persons in philosophical thought, in the past as well as today, has meant that the extent of professional writing on the subject of late is considerable. I make no attempt to review this substantial body of philosophical work, but only to refer to special aspects of it which seemed to help, by contrast usually more than by agreement, the more precise presentation of the views I wished to advance.

I hope thus that the way will be made clear for the presentation of the main views about morality and religion which I had promised earlier and which will take the form of a final volume in this series based on my Gifford Lectures at Edinburgh in 1966–68, to be entitled, as intimated earlier, *The Elusive Self and God*.

I was much helped, in correcting the proofs of this book, by two graduate students at Emory University, Mr Daniel Metzler and Mr Douglas Saenor. Mr Saenor also compiled the index. I am very grateful to both these gentlemen for their kind help — and to Emory University for making it possible.

I have already, in the preface to *The Elusive Mind*, thanked the Unviersity of Edinburgh for all the kindness shown me there. The completion of this book brings back nostalgic thoughts of that time, and it also gives me an opportunity to apologise for the delay, caused mainly by other writings to which I was committed, in bringing out the present volume. I hope the third volume in this trilogy will not be so long delayed.

I wish also to thank Mrs Ann Marangos, of Macmillan, for the care with which she has seen this book through the press.

30 June 1981 HYWEL D. LEWIS

1 Dualism Restated

In the first volume of my Gifford Lectures, entitled *The Elusive Mind*, I set out to show how radical is the difference we must draw between mental states or processes, on the one hand, and material or physical states, on the other, including one's own bodily states. These two processes, if I may for convenience retain the one term here, are, in my view, quite distinct in nature; and the finality of this distinction seems to me to be the essence of what is usually understood by the term dualism. This is what we find in notable presentations of dualism, as in the work of Plato or Descartes. I shall not be committed in all respects to the ways these, or similar thinkers, handle the problem — there are important ways in which the two I have mentioned differ, but I shall be found to be again following Descartes more closely than others of like stature.

Very closely bound up with any general statement of the dualist position is the problem of personal identity. This was not excluded from my discussion in *The Elusive Mind*. It could not be, as the two issues are so closely linked, especially today when the misgivings of most of the more eminent opponents of dualism centre on the difficulty of giving an account of personal identity, including of course continued identity, apart from bodily continuity. These were the themes which I took up more expressly in two interim volumes, *The Self and Immortality* and *Persons and Life after Death*. They were also discussed in a publication printed for private distribution by Emory University, *Mind and Nature* which contains papers by gifted members of the advanced seminar I conducted there, as visiting Professor, and some replies to criticism by me. It is with the question of personal identity, rather than the general issue of dualism, that I shall be concerned in this volume, although the two cannot be kept altogether apart. In this chapter I set out again the main features of the position I try to maintain.

My first observations refer to a very elementary matter, though

1

one about which it is also very important to be clear. In its most downright or unambiguous form materialism means that we just cannot recognise any reality which cannot be exhaustively described in material or bodily terms. This was the view defended, in a very uncompromising form by the late J. B. Watson whose book *Behaviourism* became somewhat celebrated for some time after its publication. It has the considerable merit of being unambiguous. On this view, my thoughts just are the processes that go on in my body, including my observable behaviour; and if I sit quietly to ponder, as I am doing now to consider a philosophical question, this can be described exhaustively in terms of incipient movements of my vocal cords; my anger is the tension in my breast, my shyness the blush on my cheek. The story can be told entirely in these terms, and there is no need to refer at all to any further life of the mind or any inner or private experience.

Few thinkers have the boldness to subscribe openly to this position today. But whether others have managed to avoid it as completely as they thought remains a moot point, as I tried to show in *The Elusive Mind*. Professor Gilbert Ryle was as firm in his rejection of materialism as of dualism. 'A plague on both your houses' was his strain. The great mistake was to try to take sides on this issue of materialism versus dualism. We need neither -ism. We can dissolve the difference between them by adopting a completely different approach. Whether he succeeds is another matter; admirers of Ryle's work and adherents to his view are apt to stress the innocuousness of it, in relation to our main concerns. He was not saying anything that should worry us. Of course, they say, we think and become pleased or angry and enjoy works of art and fine friendships. It is not disputed that we have intelligence, and that there are standards of excellence to be striven after. Was not Ryle a master of English style himself, and how could this be, and how could he have been one of the most famous editors of our time if he did not have exacting standards of literary and intellectual excellence? Even so, when we look closely at what Ryle actually says about intelligence and purpose, it is very hard to see that there is any difference of substance between his position and the less ambiguous 'old-fashioned' materialism which he castigated also. When we read that the surgeon's skill consists 'in his hands making the correct movements', have we travelled that far from the more lurid and less subtle behaviourism of J. B. Watson?

On this head I shall add nothing to what I have said in the

earlier volume[1] where I have tried to show that not only Ryle but many others cover up with subtlety and a bold affectation of innocuousness what remains in essentials a materialist repudiation of any reality which cannot be exhaustively reduced, in the proper analysis, to dispositions of physical matter.

To those who remain undaunted by such comments, or who have no qualms about adhering to a frankly materialist view I add, to the comment that this flies in the face of all experience — the pain as felt is not the set of physiological conditions by which the dentist or others may account for it, however exhaustive at that level — I add that it makes nonsense of all our concerns and aspirations. Nothing seems to matter if there is merely physical existence. Ryle may have had exacting standards in literary presentation of philosophical views, but have these any meaning or significance if we have no proper appreciative awareness of them? Ryle would not deny this, but it is hard to reconcile with his philosophy of mind.

I should like to put the present main point very starkly in the following way. A colleague of mine in my early days of teaching, a promising economist, had become an ardent communist. He gave up his post and spent many years in Russia. In due course he returned on a lecture tour. I heard two of these lectures. One was in praise of all the social conditions he had witnessed in Russia, improved housing conditions, better physical amenities, better education, better arts and theatre and so on. The second lecture was a defence of outright materialism which the speaker at least thought to be the proper understanding of Marxist communism. I still remember the bewilderment of his audiences as they sought to reconcile the themes and spirit of the two lectures. Assuming that the first could be accepted without qualification, what importance could it have if the second was sound? What does better education, or better housing, or better theatre mean if we are dealing with strictly material reality? Inanimate matter does not require to be properly housed, and it cannot enjoy a work of art or a joke. But once we pass to the level of at least some sentient existence, we have questions of worth or significance which acquire their more distinctive importance as we move up the scale to more rational consciousness. But in all this we seem compelled to recognise some reality which cannot be itself described in strictly physical terms, however close the involvement may be with material conditions. It is for these reasons that we speak of cruelty to animals but not to pieces of wood or stone. I may misuse a stone or spoil a fine piece of sculpture which many may enjoy. If, in a fit of temper, I vent my spleen on a chair or table which I beat with my stick, I may be arraigned for the folly of ungovernable rage, or for wanton destruction of valuable property, but hardly for cruelty. If I beat my dog in the same way I am certainly cruel, just because the dog will feel the pain of the blows as the chair cannot, except in obviously high flights of fancy or sentiment.

This is the obvious divide from which dualism takes its course. At some point we have to recognise an 'inner' experience, not literally inner but only in the sense of being privately and immediately felt or apprehended. In the long history of our planet, and for all we know of other heavenly bodies if we could discover them, a point must have been reached where, out of dispositions of non-sentient physical matter, there emerged — how or why need not concern us now — an entirely new ingredient of sentient existence, and the same is true of each of us individually. One has no reason to suppose that an unfertilised ovum or the sperm which reaches it has any kind of sentience. Nor presumably does that come about at the early stages of pregnancy. But at some point, presumably before actual birth, it must happen. It has certainly happened by the time a young creature is born, whether it be from a womb or a chrysalis or in any other way. The question just when — at the quickening for the offspring of mammals? — is one we must leave mainly to the scientist, not because it is an exclusively scientific question, but because no one but the scientist can provide the detailed information on the basis of which we judge that we have the sort of reaction which cannot be reasonably explained independently of some presumed sentient experience. It may in some cases be exceptionally difficult to draw the line, and mistakes may be made or judgements revised. What seemed to call for an explanation in terms of a sentient factor may be found, on further knowledge or understanding, to be explicable in other ways. The philosopher as such cannot settle this. He can only affirm, as I am doing now, that at some point response and behaviour ceases to be reasonably explicable without recourse to some element of at least sentient existence. The mystery of how the change comes about is another matter. The most that I wish to insist upon now is that, however fully we may come to understand the conditions within which the change comes about, we just have to recognise a radically new ingredient.

The novelty, I must insist, is not impaired in the least by the fullness or consistency of the understanding we may have of the conditions from which it emerges. What matters is that it is new and incapable of being accounted for plausibly in the same terms as the physical explanation which was exhaustive up to that point. Certain reactions suggest and in due course confirm or require some response induced by some kind of sentience. At further stages this becomes more obvious and more complicated. For the present it must suffice to note the emergence, out of physical conditions and for all we know invariably in that way, of a responsiveness which it is not plausible to explain in terms of physical stimuli which do not induce some form of sentience.

There are few, I imagine, who would seriously dispute this today, and not many who have disputed it with consistency in the past. Persons who, in some respects, appear to be strict materialists will be found also to be appealing to factors which have no significance in purely material terms. If Hobbes was a materialist — or at best an epiphenomenalist — he has left this far behind in the highly rational persuasions by which he advises us to seek peace and avoid all the tribulations of 'the state of war'. It is only as conscious creatures capable of being moved to action by appeal to what we privately apprehend and feel that considerations such as those advanced by Hobbes have any relevance.

But once this is granted, indeed even if we go no further than epiphenomenalism, the divide has been crossed. However averse we may seem to be to a dualist view, however much we may forswear or denounce it, we have granted what is essential and set ourselves on a course which can only be consistently followed in properly dualist terms. To those who question this we must present the challenge — do they seriously deny that there is an ingredient in our behaviour, and in that of other creatures, which it is not plausible to reduce to purely physiological terms? Do we not feel pain, do we not perceive coloured entities, whatever their status, do we not hear sounds? And however full the explanation may be at the physical and physiological levels of all that occurs in this way, there is also, over and above all that, something vital for the proper understanding of such situations. This is where the dualist takes his stance. It does not complete his story, but once the initial distinction is granted, we have conceded the initial vital step from which all the rest is developed. But is there any way in which we can avoid taking this step and retain any philosophical credibility?

It is these considerations that make it so irritating to find so many gifted and eminent philosophers simply taking it for granted from the outset that there is something obviously and radically wrong, something not even philosophically respectable any more, in what is sometimes described, not inappropriately, as 'the Platonic-Cartesian way' — much though Plato and Descartes may differ in certain respects. Can we avoid taking this way once the radical nature of the distinction between mental processes and physical processes has been admitted, whatever further close relations between the two we may also want to stress. We have come down on the dualist side of the divide and must guide our further steps accordingly.

To this the reply is apt to be made — and this will bring us to a point of great importance for all that follows — that the dualist, in the present concern as in others, is simply taking his stance dogmatically and not presenting any rational case for this initial step he so confidently takes. He takes no account of recent advances in physiology, or of changing views about the ultimate constitution of the external world as the scientist presents them. In fact he offers no argument at all, he offers a dogmatic affirmation in lieu of a philosophically reasoned case. Over and over this complaint has been made recently, and as often persons like myself have made the same reply. No argument is offered because the only appeal that can properly be made is to our own experience of what it is like to be sentient or conscious in some further way.

This is the point I have taken up on various occasions, but especially in chapters 1 and 2 of my *Persons and Life after Death*. I have urged that a point is bound to be reached, in philosophical as in other controversy, where one can do no other than affirm that this is just what seems to me to be the case. There are ultimates about which it is not possible to reason further. This does not mean that all talk and further consideration is at an end. There is much that we can say round and about our 'ultimates'.[2] We may also find that we have sometimes to reconsider our position when we invoke them. But it seems also inevitable that a point should be reached, in our attempt to understand ourselves and the world around us, where we can only affirm that certain things are as we claim them to be.

This is a position where I find myself in close agreement with a saying of Wittgenstein — often quoted by his close disciples like Norman Malcolm — that philosophers must 'know when to stop'. It is unfortunate that we often stop earlier than we should or in the wrong places, and I have myself complained of the way Malcolm does this in his discussion of dreams. These, he holds, are not any kind of occurrence during sleep; neither are they waking states. What then are they? Here we are told that nothing further can be forthcoming; there is no more to say. This seems most unsatisfactory. We may also be irritated in the same way by some forms of 'ordinary language' philosophy. There are obvious (and fascinating) problems of perception arising from the familiar endlessly varying perspectival distortions in normal as much as in abnormal perceptions of the world around us. Things do look small in the distance and red with coloured glasses. We hardly ever have quite the same perception of any object. There are many different philosophical ways of accounting for this, and they do not concern us here, but it is also philosophically disturbing to be told that we need say no more than we say for day-to-day purposes when we observe that someone is 'sitting on a chair', not on an assemblage of sense-data, or that we watch horses at the races, not patches of colour.

In like manner, I have objected to the procedures of Cook Wilson and some of his followers in claiming too readily, and incidentally in ways that influenced subsequent common-sense philosophy more than is usually realised, that we know certain things without further reason. This claim in itself is, I think, amply justified — it is what I am insisting upon myself. At the same time, once made, it can be invoked too readily and without warrant. There is no case, in my view, for the insistence, made by thinkers as far apart in other ways as R. I. Aaron and Martin Buber, that we know other minds in this immediate way; nor do we have immediate awareness of the existence of an external world other than that of our own presentations as they come; much less (as John Baillie drawing on Cook Wilson affirms that we do) do we have an immediate assurance of the presence of God. Our apprehension of causality may have, in our final reflections, an element of intuitive awareness, but this is not found directly in particular causal relations as we discover them. There is, in my view, an intuitive factor in ethics at some point, but it was invoked far too easily by those like W. D. Ross and other

'Oxford intuitionists', as they are called, when they ascribed an inherent bindingness, in some measure though capable of being over-ridden, to duties to keep promises or tell the truth irrespective of the good which this practice achieves.

One may also stress the deep reluctance of any philosopher to manoeuvre himself, or be manoeuvred, into a position of seeming dogmatism and reluctance to argue and discuss his claims. Nothing would be less compatible with philosophical procedure. Even so, there is more than argument involved. We do not reason the world into existence. We seek the best understanding we can have of the way things are, and at some point, to be very carefully considered before we claim to reach it, we must just affirm that we find things to be this way or that. Philosophical skill depends a great deal on the way we manage our reflections in this particular respect.

This is the point that is reached when someone affirms that my thoughts and sensations are themselves some feature of observable reality, such as some state of my body. To take again the most simple example, if I have a pain this is something which I individually feel, it just cannot be resolved into the physical factors which cause me to feel it, even when the physiological story is told in the greatest detail from my cut finger to the state of my brain. Nor is the tale completed when note is taken of my reaction to the pain or of my disposition to act in certain ways, such as putting on a plaster or visiting the doctor. The pain itself is none of these things, whatever the significance of the further factors noted. The pain is altogether different in itself and can only have its peculiar existence in my having it. Likewise my thoughts and other experiences. My perceptions at the moment, however conditioned by states of my body and the factors which affect them, have no observable or extended character. No one perceives my perceiving the walls of this room in which I write. They can see me seeing the wall, but this is a rough way of speaking perfectly adequate for normal purposes. No one strictly sees my seeing, and the thoughts I am trying to express are not themselves of the same order of being as the marks on the paper or any sounds I make. No one strictly observes my thoughts. Others may learn about them without delay, especially if I am talking, or they may judge what they are like with much closeness from my demeanour and their knowledge of me, and so on. But the thoughts themselves are not locatable in my body or anywhere else. I know them to be radically different in character from anything that can be so located or observed. It is not that they are exceptionally hard to observe or discover, like something well hidden or inaccessible, they are inherently the kind of things of which observation is not possible, and this I know in the very fact of having them.

If, then, all this is denied, I can only confess complete mystification; if my opponent tells me that his perceiving the white tablecloth is white or itself extended in some fashion, or that his other thoughts and mine are open to inspection in the same way as we observe external things, I know not how to answer him. For what he affirms is in the most direct contradiction to what I myself find to be the case in having thoughts and sensation of any kind, or any experience. To be told that these are, in themselves, of the same general nature as the reality I apprehend in perception is as bewildering to me as it would be if someone claimed that twice two is five. In the latter case I would assume that there was some misunderstanding, that the speaker did not know the language properly, or that he was jesting, or that he was making a supposition which he knew was false in order to work out in some fashion the implications of its being true, such as that if the multiplication is repeated the answer is ten, not eight. But I do not know what it would be for an intelligent English person to affirm seriously that twice two is five. I could make no sense of such a claim.

In precisely the same way I can make no sense of the affirmation that my experiences are observable when I immediately find them to be otherwise in the very process of having them. When challenged to produce an argument for my view there is nothing to which I can turn, any more than I could if it were seriously claimed that twice two is five. This is not because I am inept or not ingenious enough, but because from the nature of the case there is nothing which can be said. In the case of the alleged observable character of thoughts themselves, my initial assumption is that there is some misunderstanding, that the claim in fact refers to physical factors which are in some way bound up with my having these thoughts. If the matter cannot be resolved in these terms, there appear to be no other considerations that will avail.

It might be thought that it is unreasonable in these matters to generalise about what thoughts, emotions, and sensations etc. are like in all instances from what I find them to be in my own case. What right have I to speak here for my neighbour? Perhaps, in his case, thoughts are coloured, extended, etc. To this I must reply that, in finding his observable behaviour such that I must attribute it to his having certain thoughts and intentions, I am ascribing to him precisely the same kind of state as I find myself in in having any kind of experience. If he persists in affirming that his thoughts are movements of his vocal cords or that they have literally a round shape and a green colour, I can only conclude that I am either dealing with someone who is being perversely and provokingly dishonest or with some physical entity which by accident, or contrivance (presumably the latter), has been so framed as to simulate the behaviour of an intelligent being, a very elaborate answering machine.

There is in fact always the possibility of being confronted by such artefacts. We are in any case taken in sometimes by dummies or by optical illusions whereby we take a piece of wood or a stone to be a person until we are able to examine it closely. With enough ingenuity a physical entity might be contrived to simulate intelligent behaviour in a very sustained way. People have long been apt to mistake the call of a bird on occasion for a human voice, and devices which simulate bird songs in our woodlands for entertainment or a scientific purpose may often mislead both the birds and ourselves. Usually one soon discovers one's error, but science fiction would not find it hard to present an invasion of our planet by 'creatures' sent from some region of outer space to simulate the behaviour of intelligent beings, though in fact they had just been programmed or monitored to do so. It is hard to believe that this sort of deception would go undetected for a long time. But in theory one supposes that it might do so.

Theoretically there is in fact the possibility that one is always deceived in this way, that not even our closest friends and acquaintances are real persons with a proper consciousness like oneself. Presumably one would have to ascribe this to the machinations of some further superior mind, a demonic one it would seem. Or we might suppose that things had just worked out that way in the natural course of things. Solipsism, in this form, can never be theoretically ruled out. But no one in fact is worried by this possibility. We have no reason to take it as any serious threat to the way we all of us take things to be and our view that normally (that is when not subject to some trick or delusion) we are dealing, in what we regard as our relations with one another, with other persons like ourselves. We have no reason to suspect that a demon is deceiving us, and the supposition that in the physical course of things there have come about vast numbers of physical entities whose behaviour simply simulates sentient or intelligent animation like my own, but nothing else, and does this to perfection, my argumentative 'friend' or his cat 'stalking' its prey in the bushes — all this is so infinitely improbable that no one takes any serious heed of it.

At the same time it is a matter to be well heeded that, in all this confident assurance, the only immediate assurance of experience, and of what it is like, that we ever have is one's own. The ascription of thought, sensations etc. to others comes about normally with ease and spontaneously, and even when we are uncertain what other people feel and think, this concerns the particular course of their thoughts, or whatever is involved, not whether they are persons having some kind of experience in essentials the same as experience is for us. Scepticism of the latter sort only arises in the unusual circumstances where I suspect some optical illusion or its like, as when I have not had a chance to inspect a distant object closely enough to determine whether it is a man or a scarecrow or a small bush and so on. But we do not, at any time, *have* the experiences of others or know them in the same way as they do themselves in having them.

The notion that other minds or persons are known only in a mediated or indirect way has always been a source of misgiving to many philosophers (and others), not least in our own time. Cook Wilson's famous jibe about not caring to have 'inferred friends' has often been quoted, and many have made this insistence, namely that we must surely know our friends in some respects as certainly as ourselves, the basis of their rejection of dualism. I *see* my friend and am as convinced of his existence, and of much else about him, as of anything else. In some respect this is beyond doubt. I can assure people with every confidence that I have just seen my friend. There may be no room for serious doubt. Nonetheless, the position as it stands is over-simplified.

However firm I may be in my conviction that my friend is present and addressing me, I still only know this by seeing his body and hearing his words, or by some like observation. I know nothing about him, not even his existence, in the same way as I know my own thoughts and sensations in having them. I do not know what I myself think by listening to myself, or catching the look in my eye, or noting how I wince with pain. There is no step beyond having the pain and being aware of it. I am aware of it in having it, and to this I shall return shortly. But I shall not repeat in detail the arguments advanced by me elsewhere[3] against the supposition that one kind of thing can only be known in one kind of way, and that our knowledge of other persons must therefore be a paradigm of all knowledge of persons, including oneself, and committing us to the view that there is a bodily ingredient in all knowledge of ourselves. Nor will I go here into the answers, presented by me and others a great deal already, in rebuttal of the alleged difficulty, on a dualist view, of establishing the cor-relations supposedly required initially between mental and physical processes. For our initial basis is not the observed cor-relation but the assumption of intelligence, at some level, as the only plausible explanation of the behaviour we observe.

But while this is well-trodden ground now, though much over-looked by those who should heed it most, it is worth stressing at this point how much the insistence on further argument for dualism, and the reluctance to accept the appeal to the way we know what experience is like in having it, comes about from the confusing conflation of our knowledge of our own experience with that of others. If the appeal is made to our awareness of ex-perience in general, and thus focussed on the experiences of other persons, there is clearly something wanted beyond the invocation of there being experiences. For we know nothing directly about the nature of experience in the imputation of it to others. Some-thing more must be said, and this, it is assumed, leaves the matter open. There are various possibilities, which might include identi-fying experience with states of the brain.

This is, however, just what is precluded when it is insisted that the very ascription of experience to others depends essentially on the initial awareness we have of what experience is like *in one's own case*. This is where the appeal to experience, and what it directly discloses begins. One is not normally conscious of that, in the sense of reflecting upon it and carefully making deductions. It all happens so easily and spontaneously, that we rarely pause to consider it. Even so, we could have no notion, from observed behaviour or in any other way, of what it is like to think or have sensations and so forth, did we not in the first instance know all this beyond any shadow of doubt in one's own case. That is where we start, and it is at this point that we have to be content with reporting what in fact we find to be the case without requiring, or being able to supply, any further argument.

This, then (as I have insisted almost *ad nauseam* elsewhere but not unavoidably in the present state of the subject) is where we start. To those who require an argument, or who simply deny, directly or by implication of other things they say, that mental states are not radically different in nature from observable reality and incapable of being understood, in essentials, in the terms of the explanations we offer of physical processes, we can only reply by urging them to reflect again on what each one finds mental processes to be like in having them. But, while this is the essential starting point, the divide, most dualists take their case beyond this in very important ways. These must also be noted in our general survey before we take a further look at some recent attempts to refurbish the case against dualism.

The position, as outlined hitherto, would be consistent with epiphenomenalism or some form of psycho-physical parallelism or, more plausibly, with the view that all that goes on, as distinct mental processes, is determined exhaustively at all points by bodily states; and that thus, for all practical purposes, all we require to consider is the way in which the closed physical order of things operates and brings about in its train the mental states or experiences which we normally consider to be of most importance in our existence. But most dualists go far beyond this. They deny that mental processes are exhaustively determined by physical ones and extend to such processes both an inner determination of their own and an efficacy in the external world.

No one seriously denies that under the conditions which we know, there are persistent and vital physical conditions of all mental states and processes. Our bodies have the utmost importance, at least for all our present existence; they make possible, in a variety of ways, the experiences we enjoy, including the more rarefied intellectual ones. The most obvious example is perception. I am now looking out from my window over a most pleasant country scene of fields, trees and large birds flying about, and I take in also, in an occasional glance, the table on which I write, and also the sheets of paper before me, my hands holding my pen. If I move my head around I see more of the furniture of the room. None of this would come about if the retina of my eye were not affected by these objects, whatever we finally affirm their status to be, or if they changed, in which case, sitting at this window, I would see something else. The complete story would take account of the relaying of the stimulus from my eye to the brain, although we do not normally have any awareness of this. The actual seeing ensues, but made possible by the physical conditions noted.

It does not follow, however, that, even in the fairly simple (for this purpose) matter of perception, all that is involved in my seeing this particular view is accounted for by the physical stimulation of the eye and in due course the brain. For I would not see it in the present perspectives, and with understanding that I am looking at birds and trees, for example, did I not also conjure up the meaning of those objects which is not directly given in the immediate presentation brought about by the stimulation of my eye; and while there are further physiological conditions of this further fullness of the way in which I view the scene, the mental process of entertaining meaning and grasping its implications is a distinctive feature of that *sui generis* process itself. The course of experience moves, in large measure, in terms of what experience itself is like, and here again the final consideration must be, not any peculiarities or complexities of brain and neurological processes, or any similarities they may present to structures of thought and experience, but our own appreciation of what experience essentially involves.

This becomes more obviously evident in our more severely intellectual activities. Our thoughts are not exhaustively rational, we often blunder and become more confused and less coherent and consistent than we would like, and we point this out to one another in discussion and argument. But this gives us no grounds for doubting or denying that the distinctive determinant in all our thinking is the inherent connection of ideas through reason or association and image. Our thoughts normally take their course from the way they themselves expand and lead on to other thoughts. The reason why I think as I do now is that this is the course which my own ideas take or prescribe for themselves. This itself would not be possible, in the conditions we know, without the due functioning of my brain. A failure in the brain, even a small one, can bring my thinking to an end or make it incoherent. Even the stuffiness of the room can make a difference. At the same time the physiological conditions only make possible a different and distinct activity which proceeds mainly in terms of what it itself is like. To question this would be to bring into complete and immediate jeopardy all the activities to which we attach most significance. It would certainly be at variance with all we normally suppose. I reason with my friend because I assume that this may directly influence what he also thinks.

Indeed, it is hard to understand the zest and even pride with which some severe materialists press their case when this itself involves the repudiation of the force of argument as such to modify the course of our thinking. They would have to have recourse to procedures like the ones noted above where any distinctness of thought and experience was denied. Sooner or later we have a *reductio ad absurdum* of the desperate repudiation of what is so obvious a fact of experience.

The dualist further maintains, however, in the third place in this context, that not only is thinking largely the determinant of its own course, and likewise other modes of experience, but also that experience, in various forms, but especially in the deliberate setting of ourselves to accomplish things, or intending, makes a difference to the course of events external to such experience itself, in the external or physical world. External events influence 'inner' ones, and they in turn influence the world around us. In more technical terms, there is interaction of mind and body.

This normally takes the form of affecting the course of external events solely by directly influencing one physical entity, namely one's own body. It is a moot point whether there are any exceptions to this, or causation at a distance as it would normally be. It is alleged that, in some paranormal occurrences, even if there is physical contact, as in bending a fork by gently rubbing it, we do not have the normal causal effect of our bodily states on events beyond them, but the immediate influence of our minds on other things than our bodies. A vivid example would be the successful willing of a book to leave the shelf and come to my hands. There is no inherent reason, as far as I can see, why there should not be such exceptions to the normal processes, and investigations are conducted on the assumption that they may at least happen at times. But if they do happen, they are certainly very exceptional and limited. I cannot fell a tree by just willing that it should crash, or magically transfer myself instantly to my college room by willing that I should be there. The world would be a very different place if this were not the case.

Normally then — and as many would hold, invariably — a man (or a brute) becomes effective in the external world by first bringing about some change in his own body. This need not always involve effecting the changes which lead directly to the further course of things we intend to come about. I may extend my arms to take hold of an axe and swing it to fell a tree, or push back my chair, or walk to the shelves to get a book. But I may just as well utter some sounds or make marks on paper which will convey to others my wish or my instructions to them to bring the same result about for me. That is how we accomplish most that we want, communicating and doing things for one another. I stop a taxi to take me to my destination, or I send for a plumber or give orders to the waiter. But in all this the initial step must be to bring about some change in my own bodily state, if only to utter sounds which others may understand.

The effect which my mind has in this way on my body and thereby on other things is usually deliberate or intended. But states of mind may influence one's body in other ways also. The heart beats faster when a person is very excited, a man becomes pale or he faints if he is frightened, the thought of food makes one's mouth water. We turn and toss, and sometimes even walk, in our dreams. The dog's leg twitches and he whines as he lies asleep on the mat. But the normal and important way in which we bring about bodily changes is by intending or willing them.

We learn from experience what are the changes we can bring about in this way. Experience tells me that I cannot move things at a distance, but experience also teaches me that I cannot, to save my life, leap across a large chasm or fly to the top of a mountain, or even to the top of the stairs. We learn early what we can do and cannot do, and we acquire new skills like walking or balancing ourselves on a bicycle. Within the familiar limits we bring things about with ease. We may extend our powers, as when we learn to run a little faster, but the limits are fairly clearly defined, and within these we find that all we have to do is to set ourselves to bring about what we want. This usually happens without special effort or strain.

This is one of the central themes which the opponent of dualism must reject. It is difficult to see why he should want to do so. It seems to fly in the face of the plainest facts of experience. I have just lived through the experience of writing these words. I could see the page and the pen in my hand, and set myself to make the appropriate marks on the page in accordance with my train of thought. All this came about as I was intending it. Likewise when I pushed back my chair or cleaned my spectacles or stood up to get a better glimpse of something outside. The movement that I intended came about with ease at every stage as I had expected. To suppose that there is in fact no causal connection between my state of mind and the ensuing events appears to be a very bold undertaking. There are, indeed, well-known problems about causality in general, and especially the alleged necessity of causal relations. But if these are not thought to be deadly in one sphere, there seems to be no reason why we should reject them in any other. We learn about actual causal relations from experience, although, once the general way of things is known, we can deduce much without immediate observation, and we can account for events in terms of wider principles of the way things happen. But in the last resort it comes down to what we find to be the case; and the regular implementation of what we set out to accomplish, on the basis of what we have learnt to expect as within our powers, appears to be as well-established as any causal continuity.

There is, in this case, as in the earlier one noted above, a remote possibility of delusion, but it is as remotely improbable in this case as in the other. Unless we are to be committed to some radical scepticism in general, there appears to be as little ground for doubting the efficacy of the mental process of setting ourselves to accomplish things bodily as of any other causal sequence. The relationship seems to be as firmly rooted in common day-to-day experience as in any other; and, as it seems so basic to all that we assume in the normal conduct of our lives, it is a source of amazement that anyone should seriously doubt it.

If it is doubted on the grounds that the mental event is not itself as distinct and *sui generis* as is supposed, then we are back with matters already discussed. The appeal is again, as was stressed, to what we find to be the case; and if, as I have insisted, it must be sustained, this applies as much to our constant setting ourselves to bring things about physically as to any other mental process. Granted this, it appears to be a matter of simple common sense to admit that we do make ourselves effective in the world in accordance with the way we mentally set out to do so. My hand and my pen would not have moved as they did independently of my state of mind.

In seeking to counter this, some thinkers today take the line of saying that of course we bring things about by intending to do them, nothing as foolish is being held as making us out to be puppets or machines. Our thoughts and purposes count, the non-dualist is as innocent of shocking common sense as any, in fact he takes his stance as much as any on what we normally think and say, but it all needs further examination — and it is at that level that we discover that what seemed to be the operation of distinct mental events on matter of a totally different nature is in fact one process which is basically physical — or physical and mental at the same time.

This is a hard line to counter, since it seems to be giving away something which it is also conceding at the same time. It can be very tantalising when it is met. But we simply cannot have it both ways. In my other writings I have addressed myself to many of the ingenious recent attempts to sustain this ambiguous non-committal position. I discussed the attempt of Gilbert Ryle to account for purposing in terms of dispositional determination of our conduct, the appeal to what we normally say, the claim of Feigl and others that, as science is allegedly establishing a stricter correlation of brain states with mental events we can, for all purposes that matter at least, consider them to be equated and look forward to the time, comfortably put rather far, when any gap in the course of physiological events, or any variation which has to be ascribed to some other source, will have been entirely closed. The latter however remains a mere (and remote) expectation, and in the meantime we have all the evidence of our normal experience and suppositions to make it improbable in the extreme. If all that we seem to be immediately aware of, as our distinct experience, is reduced to the firing of nerve fibres or some other electrical activity, we have again to insist upon the plain deliverance of our awareness of what the mental process is like in having it.

Time would be wasted to go over these arguments again. It is for those who make the moves in question to indicate more precisely how the familiar criticisms, made by many besides myself, are to be met. Until they do so we must rest the case largely as it has been stated. But before proceeding to a further and equally fundamental feature of traditional dualism, namely the ascription of our mental processes to some entity, self, soul, substance, however named, which persists through all changes of our experience and is vital for a full account of them, I would like to pause and supplement what I have said elsewhere, in rejection of the more downright identification of mental states with physical ones, with some consideration of further recent and very influential attempts to call in question the appeal to what in fact we find our experience to be like in the very process of having it.

2 Some Recent Objections to Dualism

The case I have presented hitherto depends altogether on the adequacy of the appeal I have made to what I presented as the awareness of what an experience is like in the very process of having an experience. But this has itself been subjected to much critical comment of late. One of the foremost writers to present such criticism is Professor D. M. Armstrong, especially in his much admired book, *A Materialist Theory of Mind*. He proceeds as follows.

He presents a general theory of mind which has much in common with the position taken up by Herbert Feigl and considered in some detail by me in *The Elusive Mind*, chapter IX. Much is owed by both writers to Ryle's ascription of central importance to dispositions. But, unlike Ryle they are reluctant to agree that the main features of mental existence can be covered in this way. There is, for Feigl, some 'direct experience itself, as lived through, enjoyed or suffered', but the logical status of this must itself be considered in relation to behavioural descriptions. The main move, it may be recalled, is in terms of 'a referent' for private states or 'raw feels' which can, in a final scientific explanation, be identified with the referent of the observables by which the world around us is known. In a similar way Armstrong claims that, over and above the dispositions, as presented by Ryle in a strictly 'Phenomenalist or Operationalist'[1] account, we must have a 'Realist' recognition of 'a categorical state', or 'states of the object that has the capacity or power'.[2] This is what the strict behaviourist must reject.

'Behaviourism concentrates on the case of other minds, and there it substitutes the evidence that we have for the existence of other minds — behaviour — for the mental states themselves. To admit dispositions as mental states lying behind, and in suitable circumstances giving rise to, behaviour is to contradict the whole programme.'[3]

20

These admitted 'inner states' are however themselves conceived in close relation to behaviour, and, while not reducible to it, are defined as 'states of the person apt for the bringing about of behaviour of a certain sort'[4] — or, as it is also put, 'the concept of a mental state is the concept of a state of the person apt for the production of certain sorts of behaviour'.[5]

I am not at all certain that I would wish to subscribe at all points to the general realist basis of this submission. The problem of qualities of external objects is a very different one from that of mental existence of which, in my submission, we have a distinctive awareness in one's own case. Nor is it clear to me that inner states of mind can be exhaustively conceived in terms of their aptitude for certain behaviour. They have other features even if these have a tendency to lead to some form of behaviour. Nor is it altogether clear what of any substance is salvaged from an exhaustive behaviourist view when the admitted 'inner' or mental state is conceived expressly in terms of its aptitude for certain behaviour. There is admittedly something behind the behaviour which is being preserved from dissolution into the behavioural story itself. But it appears to be also very tenuous and to be forced to cling very precariously to its independent reality.

The general realism of his position is however very important for Armstrong. For it enables him to ask, over and above the behaviourist account 'What are these inner causes like?'[6] In line with the earlier pronouncements of J. J. C. Smart and Antony Flew, he declares them to be 'topic-neutral', that is, beyond knowing that there are such states, as the causes of behaviour, we have no direct knowledge of them, and the question of their proper nature remains an open one to be determined by further considerations. 'Mental processes have a nature of their own, although this nature is not directly given to us'.[7] We have, in short, a half-way house between strict reductionist behaviourism and the affirmation of inner states we directly recognise as such.

What then are the further considerations by which we may learn more about the nature of 'inner states'? Here, 'no logical analysis can help us. It is a matter of high level scientific speculation'.[8] An analogy is found with the way scientists, in first regarding the gene as a factor apt for the production of hereditary characteristics, are also able to identify it further as deoxyribonucleic acid. By comparison we may conclude that the identification of 'inner states' 'with physico-chemical states of the brain is, in the present state of knowledge, nearly as good a bet as the identification of the gene with the DNA molecule'.[9]

There seem, however, to be a host of assumptions here, in particular the gratuitous assumption, shared in an earlier similar context by Feigl, that every problem must ultimately admit of a scientific solution, or be a matter of sheer logical analysis. It was understandable that such assumptions should have much currency in the heyday of new scientific progress in the immediate post-Darwinian period. But it seems to be entirely out of place today, in morals and religion as much as in concerns like the present one.

Professor Armstrong, himself, moreover, admits fully that, if there is some 'self-intimating' character of mental states or some incorrigible awareness of them, 'if introspective knowledge is incorrigible, as is alleged, then our account of the concept of a mental state is untenable'.[10] This is a fair admission, and although I would not wish to put the case strictly in terms of introspection, we have the crux of the matter here. It may well be that, if we begin with a causal account of mental states, we have to admit also that 'any statement that one thing is a cause, or potential cause, of another thing, however *arrived* at, is subject to the tests of future observation and experiment'. But even on this basis we could claim that the tests in this case involve, not just external observation, but the facts as disclosed in our own inner awareness. The real issue is whether there is some self-intimating character of mental states such as Professor Armstrong admits would at once torpedo his position. Let us then look more closely at his objections to the alleged 'incorrigible awareness of, logically privileged access to, and self-intimating nature of, our own current mental states'.[11]

We find an interesting clue to the way Armstrong and many others approach this question, in his treatment of one of the cases which he thinks might illustrate what we mean by 'consciousness' when we say 'We are conscious, we have experiences'.[12] It is the case when, driving 'in monotonous conditions', we realise that we have 'driven many miles without consciousness of the driving, or, perhaps, anything else. One has kept the car on the road, changed gears, even, or used the brake, but all in a state of "automatism".'[13] This sort of case is, in my view, far too lightly invoked by opponents of dualism. In one sense we were not aware of what we were doing, and we have not much recollection of it afterwards. But does this mean more than that we were not taking special note of what we were doing, much as we are aware of many things at a particular time without allowing this to get further than the margin of our attention or make any lasting impact. 'Automatism' is not a very apt term for this. We have not wound ourselves up, or programmed ourselves, like machines to drive, any more than when we walk home on a familiar route with very little impression of the journey. Armstrong himself admits that, in the case he considers, 'one must *in some sense* have been perceiving, and acting purposively. Otherwise the car would have ended in the ditch'.[14] But how can we perceive and act purposively without being conscious in any sense of doing so. That would be automatic, and we would crash.

Professor Armstrong contrasts the case just noted with situations where we are 'lost in thought' and with the case where we are 'self-consciously trying to scrutinise what goes on from moment to moment in one's mind'.[15] We do not, he admits, require the latter case of self-consciousness to be able to say that we are conscious of our thoughts. 'When I am "lost in thought" I am, nevertheless, conscious of my thoughts'.[16] This, then, is, for him, the crucial case.

He deals with this case by insisting that consciousness in this case 'is simply a further mental state,' a state 'directed' towards the original inner states, and as such it can also be treated as 'an inner state apt for the production of certain behaviour', and this in turn can be regarded as a state of the brain, 'a process in which one part of the brain scans another part of the brain'.[17] But of this I can only say that it does not begin to convey what we are conscious of in respect to our own mental processes in cases of deep concentration. Nor would I admit any radical difference, in regard to my main claim, between the alleged 'automatic' driving and absorbed profound thinking. We may not be concerned to note and record what we feel or think in such cases. But we cannot fail to be aware at the time of what is happening mentally, and what this essentially involves. I can be aware of this without any thoughts about my brain.

The crucial mistake, at this stage, it seems to me, is to look for some distinctive case of our mental processes involving awareness or intimation of themselves. The claim that is made however applies to all mental processes, however rudimentary.

This is what needs most to be stressed in relation to further objections made by Armstrong himself and others following his lead. He proceeds largely on the assumption, shared unfortunately by many who also seek to counter his claims, that the direct awareness we have of our own mental states is itself a further distinct mental state. He speaks, at the outset of his treatment of this topic, about 'a belief' about one's own state of mind, and such a belief is taken to involve 'a proposition about A's current state of mind'.[18] He adds that the doctrine of incorrigibility means 'that any belief we have about our own current mental state is inevitably true'.[19] This places a wide gulf between the inner awareness in question and perception. For it is always logically possible that our perceptual claims are mistaken. They may be proved to be so by further evidence available to ourselves or provided by others. But any proposition we formulate about our own states of mind is in theory, it is alleged, capable of being falsified in the same way.

In support of this contention it is first pointed out that the incorrigible knowledge we have about our mental states cannot apply to the past. 'Two events that occur at different times must be "distinct existences": it is always logically possible that one event might occur but the other not occur'.[20] Put the first event a fraction of a second ago and it is now only 'a paradigm of *empirically* indubitable knowledge'. It is only in the present that 'error becomes logically impossible'. But can the certainty, that we are in pain for instance, be logically different from one split instant to another? This at least is enough to make us 'suspect the thesis'.

In reinforcement of this it is next pointed out, as a fatal objection, that any report we make about our mental state, 'anything we say, takes time'.[21] 'My indubitable knowledge that I am in pain can surely embrace only the current instant'.[22] It cannot extend to 'the time the sentence is finished'.[23] 'Our knowledge is indubitable only while it is knowledge of the current "introspective instant"'.[24] In practice, therefore, 'it is impossible to make a *statement* of the required logical status about one's mental states. For, by the time one has finished speaking, the moment to which one was referring is in the past'.[25] 'I am in pain now' is thus logically no different from 'I have a hand now'. Both are in principle empirically corrigible.

Even if we claim that the mental state and the awareness of it 'lie within the same "introspective instant"',[26] they are still 'distinct existences',[27] and we have therefore to establish some logical relation between the two similar to that between colour and extension, shape and size. But there appears to be no such logical relation which we can specify; and, it is added for good measure, if we think of the analogue of scanning by a mechanism of its own mental states, it is evident that there must be an absolute distinction between the scanner and the scanned. 'The natural view to take is that pain and awareness of pain are "distinct existences". If so, a false awareness of pain is at least logically possible'.[28]

The root difficulty here is the initial supposition that a mental state and the immediate intimation of what it is are distinct existences, accentuated by the assumption that awareness must take the form of explicit formulation or statement. A statement, even to oneself, is a distinct existence, and in principle some fault may be found with it. The kind of thing I am liable to *say* about my pain, and even to believe, in reporting at the time, may be untrue or misleading. I may be wrong about the cause of my pain and thus mistaken in describing it as toothache. I may be wrong if I say that it is the worst pain I have ever had, or I may not be a sufficient master of language to use the right word when I say it is a throbbing pain. But however much I may be liable to mislead myself as well as others in this way, it is hard to know what is seriously intended when it is questioned that I am in some more fundamental way inevitably aware of the sort of pain I am having in the very process of having it.

This does not mean that having the pain and the awareness of the pain are strictly the same. Nor is it, in this case and that of all mental existence, a matter of a logical relation such as that between shape and size. What Professor Armstrong and others are desperately trying to do is to assimilate the case of mental processes to other existences and the way we must handle those. There is no proper parallel to one's awareness of one's own states. Our descriptions and explanations are one thing, the initial self-intimating character of all mental processes or experience is another. The *sui generis* character of mental life must not be overlooked, and what we find to be the case, in all experience, is that we just cannot fail to be aware, in the very fact of having it, of what it is essentially like, however unskilled we may be in reporting it or noting it for ourselves.

Indeed, if we may venture a counter-attack, how is Professor Armstrong so '*empirically*' certain that he is in pain when he is so.

What observations would be invoke? Will he turn to the report of other people — there is nothing obviously wrong with me, I do not in the least look like someone in pain etc.? Could this ever convince any individual that he was not in pain when he was so? It might induce him to pretend that he was not in pain, or it might distract his attention and induce him to behave as if he were at ease; and this itself could bring about a partial or even a total easement of the pain. A parent may tell a child not to think about his toothache, and this in some cases might be helpful advice. But none of this means that we could actually have a pain and not be aware of it quite independently of such evidence as others may adduce for us or of any evidence available to us more privately. What makes my own pain *empirically* indubitable to me? Surely not my own screams or contortions of limb or of face. I know it right away and beyond any shadow of doubt. What makes this a paradigm of certainty? Can it be anything other than the fact that I feel the pain, just as I am also thinking these thoughts however inadequately I formulate them in words.

There appears in short to be nothing patently evidential about our awareness of our own states of mind, and yet the certainty with which we seem to apprehend them, in normal cases at least, is about the strongest there is. If, in the last half-hour, I had been thinking of Plato's philosophy, I would normally have no doubt at all that this is what had been happening. How am I so certain? Because I have some work of Plato, or about Plato, in front of me? That need not be the case at all. I might be walking through the fields with no companion or with nothing to indicate that I was thinking about Plato rather than Kant, or about something quite removed from philosophy altogether — my next holiday. Is it seriously thought that I have some subtle evidences available to me on the basis of which I form my own judgement? What could they conceivably be that would tell me anything as precise as that I was thinking about Plato — and about some quite specific feature of his philosophy? In some cases indeed this may come about. If someone is known to be at the time preoccupied with Plato — or with Plato's views about anamnesis — then we may claim to see the familiar signs — there he goes, there is the taut look on his face, the peculiar twitching of his fingers or whatever you please, he must be deep in his anamnesis thing again. But these are very exceptional situations, and the subject, in our example, may well disavow all we claim — it was not Plato this time, and even if we remain unconvinced, the person himself would be quite certain that it was, or was not, Plato as the case may be.

Normally, we would certainly accept what a person says about himself in such matters. Are we then seriously to suppose that this comes about because of observations he can exclusively make as indications of his state of mind? If we asked him how he knew, would not the obvious answer be — 'Well, just because that is what I was thinking at the time. I have just lived through that very experience, what conceivable reason have you for supposing that I am deluding myself'? And would not this request in turn presuppose the very special private awareness a person has about the course of his own thoughts?

I am not much disturbed about the problem of the 'introspective instant', except in the sense not in any way peculiar to our present concerns, namely that it is very difficult to note generally what is strictly meant by 'the present'. But this is a general problem about the proper way to think about time. Our thoughts proceed through time like everything else in the world, and if, as I maintain, there is an initial awareness of what an experience is like in having it, this must extend through any period we care to delimit; and if our confidence extends beyond anything contemporary with the experience itself, this must surely be because we believe, with good reason, though we need not consider that now, that memory is exceptionally dependable when it refers to matters about which we have had some very recent assurance. But from where could such assurance have come in the first place if not from the continuous flow of our own experience intimating itself to itself at each stage, and thus handing on to its successors what the experience itself is like? Independently of any explicit formulation of a belief about my thoughts, much less of the supporting of this belief from independent evidence, the course which any mental process or experience takes gives me the initial awareness of what it is like which I take over into other experiences and make the basis, if there should be need, of more explicit beliefs and statements about my own mental states.

I certainly do not normally make statements to myself or others about the varied features of my experience from moment to moment. Sometimes I may do this, though without claiming at all to cover all that is happening to me. In a discussion I convey as explicitly as I can to my neighbour what I think about the subject, and I may convey, by word or gesture, to my friends my delight at all I enjoy in the course of a walk in the country. But much happens also unremarked in this way, and in the solitude of my study or a walk by myself in the woods, it is only occasionally indeed that I present anything to myself about the course of my experience in the form of explicit sentences. It is only very rarely, and usually in cases of eccentricity, that we exclaim and talk to ourselves; and while we may more often, in fantasy, talk to an imaginary listener, it is certain that it is not through such con-versation that we know what the course of our experience is like.

It is for this reason that even terms like 'self-intimating' can never be altogether adequate. 'Introspection' can be misleading in the same way. We do not, for normal purposes, observe or note or look in on our thoughts. There is no stage by which we intimate to ourselves what is privately happening to us, life would be impossible if we had to do that all the time. There could certainly be no easy flow of thinking. It is not by adopting beliefs, or making explicit statements, to ourselves or to others, that we become aware of our own mental states, but much more basically in the very fact of being in those states and having an awareness of them inviolably bound up with their being what they are at all times.

This is almost, but not quite, conceded by Professor Richard Rorty in a critical discussion of Armstrong's work.[29] He complains that Armstrong is not able to do proper justice to the alleged realism by which he seeks to give some distinct existence to mental events. For these events, he observes, tend to be dissolved, in the causal account which Armstrong gives of them, into dispositional factors of behaviour or be accorded independence solely as states of the brain of which an exhaustively physiological account may be given. What additional distinctive feature of mental states does Rorty himself, then, allow? He finds this in the incorrigibility of mental states, or, more strictly, of first-hand reports of these states. As he puts it: 'What makes an entity mental is not whether or not it is something that explains behaviour, and what makes a property mental is not whether or not it is a property of a physical entity. The only thing that can make either an entity or a property mental is that certain reports of its existence or occur-rence have the special status that is accorded to, e.g. reports of thoughts and sensations — the status of incorrigibility'.[30] 'The thesis presented is that all and only mental events are the sorts of entities certain reports about which are incorrigible'.[31]

In strictness this only applies to mental events, although we may speak also of 'mental features', such as 'beliefs, desires, moods, emotions, intentions'. But 'those mental entities which I have contrasted with mental events as mental *features* are such that our subsequent behaviour may provide sufficient evidence for overriding contemporaneous reports of them'.[32] The latter, or at least some of them, are 'almost incorrigible'. As they 'become more particular and limited and, thus, approach the status of episodes rather than dispositions, they become *more* incorrigible'.[33] 'Beliefs and desires about momentary matters tend to collapse into sensations. Short-run beliefs, desires, emotions, and intentions are less like predictions of future behaviour than like avowals of contemporaneous thoughts or sensations'.[34] This 'near-incorrigibility should be the basis for widening the realm of the mental'.[35]

The weakness of this is that it centres attention on *reports* of mental events rather than the events themselves, and it opens the door to a counter-attack, somewhat along the lines of Armstrong's problem about the 'mental instant'. It has been pointed out, by Gerald Doppelt for example in his paper 'Incorrigibility and the Mental' in the *Australasian Journal of Philosophy*[36] that reports involve complex considerations and usually take us well beyond the time at which they are made.

The position is made still more precarious by the ascription of the incorrigibility in question to the fact that, in the cases where it holds, we have no 'established procedures for resolving'[37] any doubts. This is why Rorty prefers to speak of 'incorrigible' rather than 'indubitable'. We may doubt whether something looks brown to someone but 'there is no way we can rationally decide that it *didn't* look brown in the face of the contemporaneous belief'.[38]

This is in turn made to rest, still more precariously, on 'the way we speak'. 'By phrasing our definition in terms of accepted procedures, rather than in terms of the logical impossibility of error, we leave room for the sort of change that would confirm "eliminative" materialism'.[39] The change required would be one that 'involves a shift in linguistic practice' 'Reference to mental states might become as outdated as reference to demons'.[40] 'To say that it might turn that there are no mental entities is to say something not merely about the relative explanatory powers of psychological and physiological accounts of behaviour, but about possible changes in people's ways of speaking. For as long as people continue to report, incorrigibly, on such things as thoughts and sensations, it will seem silly to say that mental entities do not exist'.[41] It comes down to 'the ontology of the man in the street' and to 'what linguistic practices are adopted by the community'.[42]

We have come a long way here from the bold realism which seemed to insist on a firm ontological status for mental events. The 'ontology of the man in the street' may be an excellent guide, but we cannot rest secure in that alone, least of all in the shifting sands of the linguistic practices of a community. Our main concern should be with our own understanding of mental events as we find them to be, and the root mistake, in the case of Armstrong himself and of his critics and counter-critics, in a spate of recent discussions of incorrigibility and its like, has been to centre attention on *reports* of mental events and some peculiarity that might make them incorrigible rather than on explicit reflection on our mental events themselves.

The main consideration at all times seems to me to be just this, that, from the nature of any kind of experience or awareness, we are directly assured that we cannot be aware in any sense, other than a dispositional one, without being aware that we are so aware; and in this direct appreciation of our own awareness it becomes apparent also that this experience or awareness is essentially distinct from any external reality and to be understood in terms of itself alone, as a *sui generis* process, however much it may be related in various ways to processes of a different nature in our bodies and the world around us.

One further feature, in Armstrong's procedures and those of his followers and critics, must, however, be noted before we leave this particular issue. It is the question of alleged unconscious mental events. The path was well prepared here by Ryle in *The Concept of Mind* where he urged, against a Cartesian view, the seeming impossibility of allowing, in terms of that view, of any Freudian claims or other ways in which other persons may come to know us better than we know ourselves. The substance of the reply made to Ryle, by myself among others, was that the Freudian doctrines and their like referred to dispositional properties or tendencies in our nature. I may think myself a bolder person than I am, or more shy, because I am not as observant here as I am of my varying states of mind or sufficiently able to note them and establish always the correct impression of what I am generally like. No one claims 'private access' to his own character; that is not open to inspection in the way a machine may be examined to determine its likely performance. The immediate and unavoidable assurance we have about ourselves concerns only our mental events as we have them, it does not extend directly to the terms in which we describe those events or relate them to one another or their causes, although the reports which are closest to those events themselves and most explicit have an initially stronger reliability.

But now it is urged that the alleged unconscious extends, not only to character and dispositions, but also to the mental occurrences themselves. These may be unconscious too, and what becomes then of the vaunted assurance we have of our mental states in having them?

To this there is only one reply. There are no, and there just cannot be, properly unconscious mental occurrences. Many seeming instances may be cited against us, as in Armstrong's own example of driving in monotonous conditions or the stock example of the clock ticking without our noticing it till it stops. In all these and a host of like examples it can well be admitted that a great deal goes on in our mental existence of which we take no particular note and which does not register in any abiding way in our lasting impressions. A short while ago I looked at my watch only to realise as soon as I had done so that it was barely a minute since I looked at it earlier. So quickly and completely had the first impression passed only to be discovered in realising that I already knew what my watch told me the second time. But this itself could not happen without my having been aware, on the first occasion, of looking at my watch and noting what it said. Many things fall in similar ways to the margin of our attention and quickly pass out of our recollection, they are not explicitly noted, and it looks as if we had not been conscious of them at all. But we must have been conscious of them, without paying much attention as our main concerns were elsewhere, for them to have any place at all in the many eddies and currents of our rich and changing experience at any particular time.

There may of course be cases, as cited by Armstrong, of pain behaviour without actual pain. A nervous patient begins to scream before the dentist has done anything to hurt him — he is all set to scream or squirm already by fear or association — or one may scream apparently while under the influence of nitrous oxide. But this admits of many explanations. The anaesthetic may not have taken the full effect expected, or the treatment may induce a dream in which there may or may not be pain, or some reaction may be initiated in the dream state which leads to pain behaviour. But behaviour is one thing, however induced, being in pain another. To affirm this is not, as Armstrong holds, 'to be the prisoner of a dogma', it is rather to be released from dogmas into open reflection on what in fact we find to be the case and to an understanding of ourselves that takes its start from such reflection.

I turn now to difficulties which some continue to feel about the second feature of dualism, as outlined earlier, namely the influence which mental processes have on at least one's own body in certain ways, and the influence the body has in turn on the course of our experience. I shall confine myself to one novel and confident form of the difficulties which philosophers today are apt to present at this point.

In his recent book, *Descartes: The Project of Pure Enquiry*, Professor Bernard Williams offers a novel version of a familiar objection to Cartesian dualism and interaction of mind and body. The initial objection is this: if mental processes and physical states or processes are so radically different in nature as the dualist alleges that they are, it is hard to see how they can in any way influence one another. There must be some community of nature to make it possible for them to act on one another.

This is the argument advanced by Professor Passmore in Chapter III of his *Philosophical Reasoning* and discussed in some detail by me in Chapter V of my *The Elusive Mind*. It may indeed seem remarkable that our intentions, non-extended and private, in the first instance, as they seem bound to be, can influence the course of things in the extended physical world, however we understand this; and it is even more remarkable that it seems to happen solely in relation to one physical entity, namely the body of the person who is intending or willing.

It is, indeed, sometimes considered likely that there is causation at a distance, and recently the claim to be able to change things by psycho-kinesis has been boldly advanced. But whether this is warranted or not, the way we normally make ourselves effective in the world, including communication of our thoughts to one another, is through some bodily change we bring about. Even if psycho-kinesis occurs it will be limited and very exceptional, and presumably this will be so for any foreseeable time.

The alleged influence of mind on body, then, is indeed remarkable. But in a way so are all other causal relations. In the last resort we can only discover what they are empirically. Admittedly we do often say that certain things are bound to happen — with these dark clouds it will certainly rain, put a match to this powder and there will certainly be a devastating explosion. But we take all this to be necessitated simply because we accept it that there is a complete consistency, subject to concomitant variation, in the way things happen in the world around us. On the basis of what we have found to be the case already, we can infer with remarkable precision what will happen in the remotest times and places. Our day-to-day behaviour, as well as fine achievements of science, presuppose this. Without it we could neither live in the world nor understand it. Whether there is also a rational justification for our confidence that our physical environment will continue, in this respect at least, to suit our convenience, is a moot point. But whatever we say on this head, the very fact of causal determination itself is remarkable in the extreme, and no less so when we discover that it takes some unexpected forms at odds with our day-to-day expectations. This may well be a factor of very great importance in any view we form generally of ourselves and the world around us, and religious persons, not surprisingly or improperly it seems to me, have attached significance to it. But, without going further into this and similar issues, we can readily see how remarkable it is that, without any inherent necessity of things being the way they are, they do in fact stand in the dependable and consistent relations which we discover.

In the last resort all causal relations are remarkable, even the most familiar. We can only accept them and be grateful, most of the time at least, that they are as they are. If there is mystery in the peculiar influence of our minds on our bodies, it is no more, in the last analysis than all causal determination. At most there is a difference of degree. The requirement of a common nature seems to be a wholly unwarranted assumption, a dogmatic claim for which no justification is offered and which could create problems also for the extraordinary varieties of change we find in the external world itself.

The oddity of a causal determination is therefore no ground, in the last resort, for discrediting it. We have just to go by what we find to be the case. We cannot reject what we find beyond doubt to be the case just because we find it remarkable that it should be that way.

Professor Passmore had noted[43] that 'the only force the mind has at its disposal is spiritual force, the power of rational persuasion'. On the other hand bodies 'can only push'. How, on this basis, we can ever accept, as we all do all the time, that 'in some sense the mind influences the body and vice versa', is never explained. It seems quite evident that my purposing to put on my spectacles or wave my hand is not itself a physical state or process. It is known in the fact of having such a purpose that this in itself is no part of locatable reality that we can observe from its shape or colour or in any other way. But if we find that this non-spatial purpose does in fact normally bring about a physical change, how can we possibly question this just because it defies further explanation. We do not reason the world into existence, we find that it is what it is; and we must accept it however remarkable it may seem to be in some respects. To wonder at the way things are should be no embarrassment for philosophers.

And now, with that in mind, let us look at the variation on the stock objection which Professor Bernard Williams brings forward. When we do will, let us say to wave a hand, all that we do will is just to wave a hand. But we all know also that the movement would not in fact take place were it not preceded by various other changes in our bodies. Muscles and nerves must function in certain ways as well, and there must be a change in the state of the brain to bring all that about. If anything goes wrong as these changes are 'relayed', as we sometimes put it, the hand will not wave. It may be the first intimation of 'a frozen shoulder' or more seriously of general paralysis or a stroke. However resolutely I will to move my arm, in these cases, nothing happens. This is common knowledge, notwithstanding that the layman only has it in very general ways, and not in the fuller form available to the neurologist and brain expert.

All the same, it is not on the basis of knowledge of this kind, even the most incipient, that we will to bring about changes like waving a hand or pushing a chair. What we will is to push the chair, to take off our spectacles etc. We do not will to bring about changes in our brains, and most of us have not the faintest notion what such changes should be, or even how our joints and muscles function for us to wave a hand. The brain surgeon has no advantage over the rest of us where waving a hand is concerned, and we would have little confidence in him if he had to remind himself what goes on in his own head before he gets on with his operation on the brain of someone else.

This, as Williams points out, is the proper purport of Descartes's own warning not to think of ourselves in our bodies as a pilot in a ship. I do not move my arm by knowing what lever to pull in the first place or what the initial change in the brain must be like. I suppose that, with sufficient knowledge, we could induce some movement in our limbs in that way. We could at least imitate the doctor by tapping a knee to make it jerk. But this is certainly not how we walk about. We just decide to walk and do so. Any further knowledge we have of all that this involves is subsidiary and irrelevant to our being able to walk about at will.

So far there is nothing to dispute. But this is also the point where Williams finds an insuperable objection to the Cartesian story. This is not because Descartes was wrong about the pineal gland etc. We can substitute for this an appropriate 'electro-chemical system' or 'any input at all of the mind into the neuro-physiological system'. But even so, 'the brain', and we might add the nervous system too, 'is not responsive to willing which has brain changes as intentional content, but only to willing which has movements of other parts of the body as intentional con-tent'.[44] If I want, of my own volition, to change my brain-state, I must start by asking the surgeon to do something to me or by doing, if we were clever enough, the sort of thing to my brain which the surgeon does. Nothing of this sort normally happens. I change my brain-state by willing to move my arm. But I cannot move my arm unless the brain-change is first brought about. That is, on the view which Williams is criticising, 'the only part of my body directly responsive to my will is one which I cannot move at will'. This is thought to be enough to dispose of the Cartesian view.

I find this argument utterly bewildering, especially in view of the confidence with which Professor Williams affirms its finality. Just what is wrong with supposing that, firstly, we learn from experience that we can bring about bodily changes, like my arm waving, by willing or setting ourselves to bring this about and that we regulate our conduct in this way, *but*, secondly, that we learn in more sophisticated thought that the change which our intending or willing actually brings about in the first place is a change in the brain from which the other changes, culminating in the waving of my arm, proceed with such rapidity as to seem virtually instantaneous. Knowledge of this kind does not induce us, or require of us in any way, to start the futile business of willing to initiate a brain change. We just carry on as before in the sensible expectation that when we set ourselves to wave an arm or put on our spectacles this in fact will happen. What we can do is just to will these things. How the result comes about, and that the process involved is much more complicated than we assume in day-to-day conduct, is quite immaterial to the normal business of all we do bodily.

None of this means of course (*pace* Ryle but not him alone) that we simply perform occasional bits of willing to jolt or galvanise our bodies into the appropriate motion like pulling the strings of a puppet. As I have stressed at some length in *The Elusive Mind*, we will in a sustained continuous way all that is required as the action proceeds. But what we will is just what we expect to come about bodily. How this comes about is no concern of ours for normal purposes. The practical importance of neurological understanding and study of the brain is for doctors to know how to treat us if something goes wrong and for us to know how best to keep ourselves fit. The story of all this is also inherently important, and I would not deny that it has relevance to philosophical questions in some way. But it does nothing to affect the basic question of what mental process or experience is like and how it effects changes in the external world.

Professor Williams has a subsidiary argument which I find very strange. He observes, firstly, that to bring about a change in my brain, short of surgery or its like, I have to bring about some other change in my body, like waving my arm. I cannot directly, in his language by psycho-kinesis, move my pineal gland or my brain in any other way. But neither can I move my hand in this way either. Just try, he says: 'We must also take account of the fact that an "external" application of willing, such as we discussed in connection with psychokinesis, is no more effective in making my arm move than it is in making my hair, or anything else, move. Put your hand next to some object, such as this book, and "will" the book approach your hand: nothing happens. Now "will", *in that same way*, your hand to approach the book. Still nothing happens. Direct application of psychokinesis is no more effective with my limbs than with anything else'.[45]

Everything turns here on, 'in that same way'. What can this conceivably mean here? I certainly cannot make the book move to my hand, but I can reach out for the book, and all that I can do here is set myself or will to do this. The rest comes about in a way over which I have no further control. If I simply stare at my hand and expect it to move in some magical way other than the process of normally willing this, then of course nothing happens. But why should we ever expect it to happen? There is no way in which I can move my arm other than by willing to do so in the normal way. Cut that out, and we have to invoke something totally mysterious which, not surprisingly, has no effect at all.

Part, at least, of the trouble here is the word 'psychokinesis'. This is the word we use when we think of the possibility of our making things move, or change in some way, without doing so bodily, like making a chair come to its place or a book from the shelf to my hand. Normally, at least, we just rule out this possibility. I can only get the book by reaching for it or getting someone to do so. The claim is sometimes made however that there are people who can do this. Perhaps they have also to do something bodily at the same time, to utter a magic formula or make a gesture or rub a fork to make it bend without applying the normal force required for this purpose. There is here the possibility that some subtle physical force is engendered which we may some day discover and learn how to use, though most of us would consider this unlikely. A stricter form of psychokinesis would be to bring about the result envisaged without any other physical intermediary. We will the book to come to our hands, and it does, like a bird to our call.

Professor Williams takes a little more kindly to the possibility of psychokinesis in this form than to the related account of how mental processes bring about changes in our bodies in the course of normal behaviour. He suspects that 'deeper consideration' will show that it 'is not merely empirically impossible, but inconceivable'.[46] But, he adds:

Let us grant, generously, that whether psychokinesis is possible is an empirical issue, including in the idea of its occurring, the idea that the influence could not be affected by any physical force, and moreover, that nothing could produce the influence

but conscious thought (thus printing out the desired result in a
near-by computer, for instance, would have no effect). With
that, we have granted some approximation to the idea that it is
not unintelligible for mind to influence matter separate from
it.[47]

This, however, subject to the 'deeper consideration' which is
not provided, is a very radical admission. What is claimed in
interactionist theory is that mind simply does influence matter in
this way, in some regards. If it is allowed to be not unintelligible,
why be so persistently averse to accepting the plain fact of
experience that it does happen? To this Professor Williams only
replies in terms of the consideration to which I have referred
already, namely that we do not will to bring about the change in
our brains which determines the subsequent physical movement.

There is, in fact, in principle, no difference between the
psychokinesis by which we might bring a book from the shelf to
our hands and that by which the act of will induces the change we
intend in our bodies. At some point the influence is direct, and
that is surely what matters. That this only happens, so far as we
can firmly establish, in the normal course of physical behaviour,
or the control of our own bodies, in no way detracts from its
eventual directness or the sheer fact that it does happen. There is
no inherent reason why there should not be further psychokinesis
— as some affirm to be the case. We simply find that it is normally
confined to control of our own bodies, and very limited at that.
This is, however, no reason at all for rejecting what we find to be
an inescapable fact of experience.

We may indeed admit that there is 'something deeply mysterious about the interaction which Descartes's theory required
between two items of totally disparate natures, the immaterial
soul, and the gland or any other part of an extended body'.[48] But
it is no more mysterious than many other things which we find in
fact to be the case, and it is somewhat unfair for this reason to
speak of 'the obscurity of the idea that immaterial mind could
move *any* physical thing'.[49] 'Obscurity' is a mildly reprobative
term, and suggests that there is something which should be made
plain. But there is a limit to explanation and a point where we
just have to accept things as we find them to be. No explanation
of ours is exhaustive, and if the world is in some ways very remarkable, we must accept that too. In fact would it not be better for

philosophers, rather than trying to explain away or discredit extra-ordinary facts of experience, to stop and wonder at them and their possible further implications.

3 The Elusive Self

I turn now to a further feature of dualism, already mentioned, and one which is, in my opinion, of altogether cardinal importance. This is the insistence that, in addition to states of mind distinct in nature from physical states but constantly interacting with them, there is also a subject, or a self or soul, which remains constant and is uniquely involved in all the flow of our mental states or experiences. This notion has a long ancestry. It appears, for example, in celebrated ways in the work of Plato, Augustine, Descartes and Kant. It is the version presented by Descartes that has attracted most attention, mainly critical, in recent times; and that is also the version which appears to me, though not adequate at all points, most satisfactory in essentials. This is also the view to which I myself subscribe and which I shall seek to present in this chapter in ways that do not seem to me open to the stock objections.

I begin with a major matter and one peculiarly difficult to handle philosophically. It may have been noticed that I used the word 'involved' in my statement a little earlier. The self is 'involved' in states of mind. Other terms which we use here are 'own', 'belong', 'have'. The states of mind are said to be 'owned' by or to 'belong' to the self. We also say at times that the self 'has' its various experiences; and critics defend, by contrast, the 'no-ownership' theory and so forth. We are here at a very difficult crux which it is important to indicate at the outset, for most of the relevant controversies hinge on whether this is adequately taken or not.

This crux concerns the way we are to understand, or to speak, about the self and its relation, to use a term for which it is not easy to find a substitute, to our particular states of mind as they occur from moment to moment. 'Relation' is a word in very common use here, and we may easily, in discussion, come across the question, 'How is the self related to its passing states?' But even this familiar term can be misleading. For, although the view being presented is that the self is not to be identified with its passing states or reduced to them, or any pattern of them, it is not altogether sound to envisage the self as entirely a thing apart to which the fleeting experiences we have stand in some special relation. The words 'own' or 'belong' are metaphors, and if they are taken very cautiously as such, as just convenient and very rough labels for something which is not being properly described at all, they may serve their turn. Strictly, the proper provenance of these terms is ethics, including here social and political concerns. What I own is my property; this pen belongs to me, I have paid for it, or had it given me by someone who had paid, I am the person to say when and how it may be used, etc. It is all a matter of the appropriate rights, of the bundle of things which I am especially allowed to do with this pen. There is nothing corresponding to this in the way my states of mind belong to me. They are not conferred upon me in any way, and do not in any other fashion have anything to do with the proper use of powers or privileges. My experience is not mine in that sense at all.

Few, if any, are in fact misled by the normally ethical or legal use of words like 'mine' or 'belong' when applied to the self and passing experiences. We just have to have some word, and while the terms we do employ can be quite innocuous when used with no peculiar commitment, as in fairly simple statements like 'I have a pain' or 'This pain was mine', meaning simply that I and no other was the one 'in' pain, they can easily become consolidated into ways of thinking that are philosophically very misleading and produce reactions seriously at odds with what seems to me the proper way of viewing the matter.

The fact is that 'relation' is a word we most commonly use in reference to items in the external world — this is to the left of that, this spoke belongs to this wheel, that is it stands in some relation to the hub and the rim or, as we may put it, to the wheel as a whole. General questions are asked about the relation of a thing to its parts, in which case we are apt to regard the whole as just the parts related in a special way. On occasion a thing or entity has been thought of as quite other than its parts or qualities, some unknown 'substratum' in which they 'inhere'. This, and like severely realist views of external objects, has never seemed to me very plausible, but for the present it will suffice to say that we must either think of relations as subsisting between a whole and its constituent parts, or between one such whole and another in a more widely embracing unity, or between parts and some un-known substance. But whichever of these views, or any variation on them, we adopt, or whatever other way we adopt of thinking about relations and affinities in the external world, this provides no proper clue to the way my experiences may be said to belong to me or to be states of my mind.

I stress this very much, for so much in the course of the philo-sophy of mind, especially of late, has been determined by our disposition to think of mental existence, and the philosophical problems it presents, in the terms which we have initially found appropriate in our view of all that we find in the world around us. Our model, quite naturally, is the external world with which, and with one another, we are directly preoccupied most of the time.

The self, I insist, is not to be identified with passing states or any pattern of these, it is an entity which 'has' them. On the other hand, it is not a something altogether apart to which they are somehow 'related'. It is altogether hard to draw that distinction between a person and his states of mind. If we do we are apt to conjure up some picture like that of beads and the string which holds them. As against this, I prefer not to ask strictly what is the relation between a self and its passing states, notwithstanding that I am quite firm in regarding the self as an entity over and above its particular states, a genuine distinct reality capable of being what it is and functioning independently of the particular states of mind it happens to have.

There is, in fact, no proper analogy to the way my states of mind are mine or belong to me. Mental existence, as I have much stressed, is radically different from external being, and the terms in which we seek to think of it and discover what may be appro-priately said about it, must not, except by very rough analogy, be borrowed from the world of external things. This does not mean that we must coin an entirely new language in speaking of mental things. We can only use the words and forms of speech that have come about in our common intercourse, and this it is which so accentuates our problems in the philosophy of mind. We must just proceed as best we can, and with an unfailing sense of caution, like people moving through a minefield, aware that at any moment we may be too rash and say things that are slanted away too much from the peculiar delicate reality with which we must cope without being reduced to totally inarticulate suspen-sion of judgement. We cannot just be silent, there are things to say, but we must all the time be conscious of the way the things which it seems appropriate to say can easily become misleading or inadequate — or be fossilised into forms where the lack of special insight and novelty converts them, in too familiar usage, into coarse representations of external things and their modes and behaviour.

This is one of the main reasons why 'the way of silence' has had such a strong appeal in the past as in recent times, in Wittgenstein's famous aphorism for example. But our situation is never quite as desperate as that. In religion there is, indeed, a special complication, in that the central concern is usually, if not always, with some reality which is transcendent or ultimate in the sense of falling altogether outside the finite system by which things become comprehensible to us. But even here we are not without recourse to reliable clues. In the philosophy of mind we are not dealing with anything that is strictly transcendent or outside the way or scheme of things properly accessible to us, though a loose use of the term transcendent has sometimes led to its use in any connection where we are not dealing with observable reality. Our minds, and what it is to be a person, is in no way a mystery occluded from us. There is nothing, in one sense, which is more open or transparent to us. But to think and speak without ambiguity about mental existence is nonetheless exceptionally difficult because the ways in which we think and speak arise in the context where our common environment has a formative part.

It is all the same important to have sound ideas in the philosophy of mind and not be wholly deterred by the requirements of estimable caution; and in this spirit we must proceed to affirm, on the one hand, that the self which has experiences is not itself some ingredient of the particular experiences themselves or any other feature of them as fleeting experiences, but, on the other hand, is the experience of having them as peculiarly its own experiences in a way for which there is no strict analogy in the relations of things or properties in the external world. There is nothing accidental or contingent in the way the pain I have is mine, or these thoughts while I think them. Neither the pain nor my thoughts have any reality except in being felt or thought by me. It can indeed be properly said that they are me, or that they belong to me, or make me myself in an indissoluble way. I cannot be separated from them as my skin and my clothes may be removed from my body. The pain hurts just because it is me being in pain. I revile my jealous or unworthy thoughts, not as things incidental to what I am, but as, in a very important sense, what I myself am. I am thinking them, I am in them in this peculiarly intimate way, they are not tagged on to me, it is me myself thinking them. Nothing could be closer, more at one, nothing less capable of being divorced than a person and his thoughts or sensations as he has them.

At the same time it is equally true that I am not just my thoughts and sensations. I remain the same me, the one being that I am, in all my other thoughts, near and remote. When, in a short while I shall have quite different thoughts, or when I have no concern or interest to recover my present thoughts, I remain the distinct person who has the thoughts in the one situation as much as in the other. It is the same 'I' or 'me' that has all the experiences, and this is not just a way of talking; I am involved in a special way in my thoughts and yet I am not just the having these thoughts and experiences.

It should be made clear, before we go further, that there is one simple sense in which my thoughts are in no way peculiar or private to me. Others may have the same thoughts or, as we sometimes put it, think along the same lines, and I may share my thoughts with others or communicate them. Sharing our thoughts is a very important part of living. But my having these particular thoughts at this time is a distinct mental occurrence, and so is your having similar (or different) thoughts, whether or not we are sharing our thoughts or in dialogue. I may have your thoughts in the sense of thinking the same as you do, or be much stimulated, in agreement or disagreement, by what you are thinking, as I learn about it. But my thinking what you also think, or in some way 'in tune' with you, is a distinct occurrence or flow of thought, your thinking it is another. I cannot have your thought or your pain in the special sense in which you are involved in your having them, and no one can have my thoughts except in the sense of thinking similar thoughts, or learning what I am thinking. Ontologically the two occurrences or flowing of thoughts are quite distinct.

This is very closely bound up with the way a thought is uniquely my thinking a thought, there just can be no thought that is not thought by some distinct person, except in the sense of an ideal or logical content, an abstraction but not an actual on-going thought being thought. There are not, in old-fashioned terms, any strictly 'floating' ideas. We just cannot seriously conceive, I submit, what it would be like for there to be just a thought or flow of thoughts that is not being had or 'entertained' by some individual in such a way that it is at the time that individual. My thoughts and sensations are strictly me and can have no ghostly existence except as they are in this way me or some other person.

At the same time, it is equally, or indeed more, important to appreciate the sense in which they are not me. They are not essential to my being the being I am. I could be having other thoughts at this moment, but it would be me having them, just as certainly, unless I perish, I shall be having other thoughts a little later and again after that. Indeed the whole course of my life may change, my interests and preoccupations may become completely different, my outlook may be new and I may find myself, as a reformed, or a lapsed, character, having very different sorts of experiences from those I have now — and yet it would, in a peculiarly final and unavoidable sense, be me, the same being, having these other experiences. Indeed, as I shall again maintain to be possible, the whole course of my life's experiences from the first moment could have been other than it is — and yet it would be me having this different kind of life, ontologically, in the strictest sense, the same person.

The key to the way we are to understand ourselves as minds or persons, or to think philosophically in a sound way about ourselves, is that we should not be daunted by the seeming paradoxes of what is now being submitted, namely that, in a very inexpugnable sense, all my experiences, as they occur, thoughts and sensations and all else equally, are what I am myself, they could not be except as me thinking etc., while, at the same time, in an equally radical and inescapable sense, I am not these thoughts but the continuous being into whose existence they come in a wholly integral way which also leaves my distinctness as the being that I am unaffected by whether I happen to have these thoughts and experiences or any other.

We may put this more simply, as I did earlier, by just insisting that the self or person is not the particular mental events that make up his life, or any shape or pattern of them, but the being, or the entity or subject, who has them and remains identical in the varied course of them. But without surrendering anything on this score, we have also to learn to live intellectually with the equally basic assurance that all our experiences, as they occur, are ourselves having the experiences in such a way that notions like 'being related to', or any but the most general use of terms like 'own' or 'belong', are singularly inappropriate and misleading. I am not related to my thoughts and pains — I have them; and I need not have them to be the uniquely irreducible being that I am. If even 'having' leaves us a little uncertain here, that is as it should be, for no terms can ever be quite satisfactory in describing a mode of being that is so radically different from all that we encounter in the world around us in which we live.

Some religious writers, pre-eminently mystics, lay peculiar emphasis on the unavoidable obliqueness of all the allusions they make to supreme or transcendent being. This is for the reason noted already, namely that they are dealing with a reality that, in essentials, is beyond comprehension. They must speak of it 'slantwise', in Evelyn Underhill's word. There is something akin to this in accounts of mental reality also, not because that is occluded from us but because of the difficulty of finding terms that do not, in this context, have misleading associations or a likelihood of becoming misleading in familiar established usage. The corrective to this is to be constantly reflecting on what in fact we find to be the case and keeping that well in mind in the way we talk to one another about it or set out our own thoughts in the most satisfactory way.

There is in this no licence for being arbitrary or simply allowing ourselves to be guided, as we have seen that some are prone to do, by what happens to be the linguistic usages of a community. We have to get behind that to what we find to be the case and, in renewed appreciation of that, adapt and vary our terms to convey the most unambiguous impression of what we find. Professor John Wisdom was right in urging us to 'be careful' but not in telling us that, subject to this, we could say 'what you like'.

We stay then with the view that, in all experience, there is a self or subject directly involved in having all the experiences which it does have and yet independent, in its own distinctness, of having any of the experiences which in point of fact it does have. It is in clinging to this notion, and setting forth more fully its implications, notwithstanding the problems presented in handling it philosophically, that we shall arrive at a sound philosophical understanding of what it is for us to be the beings or persons that we are.

I shall now try to set out in more detail how this position is to be sustained. The most immediate question is fairly obvious, namely how do we come to know that, in all experience, there is the purported 'abiding' self, and what, if anything, can we know further about it.

One of the most celebrated attempts to establish the existence of an abiding self or subject of experience is that of Kant. He maintained that we have to allow or recognise such a subject in order to account for the way we have experiences in an ordered or co-ordinated way, or as it is sometimes put, be aware of a 'world of objects' which we can understand and manipulate. If we were confined to the passing scene as it comes to us in presentations we would not be able to give it any meaning, we would see nothing in proper perspective or appreciate that the coloured surface presented to us is bound up with other properties, hardness and solidity etc., and with a vast nexus of other properties of things that make up the world in which we live and encounter one another. There are various ways of understanding the 'world of objects' which we experience in this way, ranging from the views of Berkeley and recent phenomenalists to the more realist insistence on strictly independent physical objects. These variations do not concern us now, for, on any of these views, it is hard to avoid the conclusion that the co-ordinations in our experience of the world, even at its most rudimentary stage, requires that there should be the sort of continuity which is hard to explain without the admission that we must live on in some way as the same person from one experience to another. How otherwise would we properly apprehend the passing scene or give proper significance to what our senses bring before us at any moment?

This seems to me quite unanswerable as far as it goes, and it is a submission also which has been very effectively restated by recent Kantian scholars such as H. J. Paton.[1] I have nothing to add to their own presentation of the Kantian argument in itself. But, as I have insisted in an earlier presentation of this point, in *The Self and Immortality*, the precise status of the subject established in this way remains somewhat ambiguous. Kant himself seemed to waver between various possibilities, sometimes implying that the self was no more than an 'imaginary focus', at best some wholly unspecified, possibly abstract or formal, condition of unified experience, and at other times inclining, though not very explicitly, to treat the 'pure self' as a genuine 'thing in itself', a reality which we cannot properly know, since we only strictly know objects, according to Kant, as they appear under the particular conditions of the kind of experience we have, limited it may even be to the objectivity of conditions imposed, though not arbitrarily, by our own minds — or the kind of minds we have — but all the same, 'as things in themselves', having a genuine independent reality which the limitations of our kind of experience requires us to posit. The ramifications of this kind of bifurcation does not concern us now. For what certainly emerges is that Kant is undoubtedly confined to regarding the self as something we can never properly know, however firmly and unavoidably we have to recognise or posit it as a pre-condition of our having the kind of experience we undoubtedly do have.

Some followers of Kant, Lotze outstanding among European thinkers, and fairly recent British philosophers, like James Ward and F. R. Tennant late in the last century, have expressed dissatisfaction with the limitations of the Kantian approach to the topic, and they have been quite insistent that we must supplement the Kantian argument, of which they fully approve in itself, or give it more body, by maintaining firmly, in the words of James Ward, that the subject required to meet the Kantian case must itself be 'the concrete conscious subject', not 'an intellectual abstraction'.[2] To regard persons, in the sphere of practice or that of understanding, as just 'the limit of a long process of intellection' would in his view be 'outrageous'.[3] A 'psychological fiction' or 'abstract "consciousness"' will not do.

With all this I heartily concur, but I am also convinced that we must carry the case still further, for it seems to me hard to give real substance to the Kantian argument from the unity of experience unless we allow some independent understanding of what it is to be a self or subject. For Ward, the self still tends to be known only as the implicate of object. But how can we carry the matter further without ascribing to the alleged subject the sort of concreteness which we have reserved for entities in the world around us. Once we make the self that sort of object we are in the toils of the difficulty Hume encountered, in trying to look into himself etc., for we do not observe or discover the self as we find objects over against us in the world around us, and capable of being characterised in various ways and identified on that basis. This is sometimes put in rather formal terms by saying that the subject must always be a subject and never an object. Make it an object and it is no longer a knower — it becomes one identifiable object among others. For this reason the self can never be properly known. The subject must remain just a subject.

I am not altogether happy with these last ways of putting the case, although I fully admit that they do bring us very close to the stance we must adopt. The presentation of the self as essentially subject, the knower, and never an object, smacks too much of the formalism which marks the limitations of the severely Kantian approach. It may even appear to be just a play on words. But whatever we make of that, there is certainly a major difficulty the moment we pass beyond the 'intellectual abstraction' and meet the request to indicate more specifically what sort of entity or 'something' this alleged self is found to be, and by what process does it come to be recognised or specified. What sort of 'something' is it?

There is an insidious temptation at this point to make a simple appeal to introspection or, more cautiously, to 'knowledge by acquaintance'. The main complication about introspection, for our purpose, is that it is ambiguous. In its most familiar usage it simply refers to the reasonably straightforward matter of noting our various moods and attitudes as reflected in the course of our experiences (including our own purposing) as they occur. We record, for ourselves or others, what we think or feel at particular times, and so forth. This has difficulties, for the fact of paying special attention to an on-going experience is liable to distort it, as has often been stressed, and we find it hard to be rid of bias of various sorts. But, in one way or another, with checks and counter-checks, psychologists do manage to ensure with reasonable reliability that persons can report on the way it goes for them from time to time in various situations. Sometimes the report is severely technical, as when a psychologist tests people for immediate responses to visual stimuli, and sometimes it is more general, as when we describe how we feel in situations of danger or when teased and provoked to anger. However difficult it may be in practice to 'look in on' ourselves, or observe ourselves, in this way, there is no insurmountable difficulty in principle. In some ways, this kind of introspection is something we practise all the time, the more formal exercise of it is simply more systematic or professional.

Hume would have no particular difficulty about this kind of introspection, and he would probably have come across a lot of it, to his own irritation, in the time he spent in company with the more sensitive and temperamental Rousseau. But, whatever problems this presents, and whether we think more in terms of retrospection or the immediate noting of mental states in recollection the moment they are over, the matter is altogether different when we are asking, not how does this object look to me and how many flashes of light I have seen, and not even just how angry I was when provoked or pleased to be praised, but what is it over and above this for it to be me noting the flash of light or undergoing the fear. This is 'looking in', or something like it, in a very special sense, and it was this that bothered Hume and elicited his famous repudiation of ever managing anything of the kind.

At this point we must be careful not to be led astray by being diverted into the controversy as to whether the attitudes presented by terms like 'fear' or 'pride' are already on-going states or merely dispositions, tendencies to behave, as Ryle firmly thinks that they are. On this issue enough has been said already. Whether 'pride' is a term that has more than a dispositional use is a moot point that need not detain us. It is certainly odd to speak of observing ourselves being proud. But whatever we say of the limitations and extensions of dispositional terms, it would make little sense to consider even dispositions of considerable generality without presupposing, as the basis of them, some on-going mental processes through which we pass from moment to moment. We need not take up the cudgels again against outright behaviourism. The issue now is not whether there are on-going mental states, nor even whether we can, and in what ways most successfully, record what they are like at the time or in dependable recollection, but whether we can further note and specify what it is like to be the subject involved in having various experiences and reacting to them. Does one ever observe the self *qua* self, and if so how do we describe what it is to be a self over and above having certain states of mind and anything that may be obliquely deduced from this or generalised about them.

In short, can we ever 'look in' on the famous 'pure self'? Our major philosophical impulses, and the main weight of the very tradition in which the idea of a pure self or ego is given prominence, strangely predispose us to say 'No' here. By its very purity this self is just a self. What description can we offer, has it ever been provided, in general or in particular terms? Just what is it to be a subject of experience, or an agent, which can be indicated in any terms other than descriptions of the experience itself or the actions we intend or bring about? What, to put it bluntly, sort of self is mine and what is yours? In what particulars do they differ?

In the tradition, there has been an exceptionally strong disposition to say very firmly that there can be no specifiable difference here. This, in turn, has led, very understandably, to further philosophical stances, in many cases stances to which the thinkers concerned were already much predisposed, where the finality of any distinctness of persons is rigorously questioned. Major examples of this are idealist metaphysics and monistic mysticism. The former, keeping close to the initial formalism of the Kantian procedures, tends to think of individual selves as 'centres of unification' capable of being so enlarged, like holes in a wall, as eventually to overlap with all others and disappear in the completer unity of the whole. There is nothing in a 'centre of unification' to preclude this or to single out any individual, other than in terms of the contents unified, from any other. The second, the mystical line, takes an even bolder course in dispensing with any finality of distinct persons. There is no way to discriminate, and so the boundaries and barriers melt away and each self is merged in every other or in the one Supreme Self which is all there is. Both these ways of thinking have a long and celebrated ancestry and both have, in many ways, had considerable influence.

I have elsewhere[4] stressed how grievous are the consequences, for a great deal that is of worth and importance for us, of subscribing to either of these types of final philosophical view — or their religious counterpart. I shall return to this elsewhere. In the meantime these wider ramifications of our problems do not directly concern us here. For the immediate issue is whether anything can be said about a self or subject, or what it is to be a subject, which will make further discourse about it intelligible and show us how we are to distinguish one such self from another. If we cannot do this, we seem, on the face of it at least, to be in serious trouble.

Let me now make it very clear, and come to the crux of this matter, that I do not propose to offer any positive answer to the understandable request I have been noting. Just what could one say? What is it to be me, rather than you, other than my dis-

positional tendencies or the particular course of my own history —
or my body. It is these considerations that have driven so many
contemporary philosophers either to surrender altogether the
notion of self-identity and seek some substitute, or to give an
account of it, with ever-increasing desperation it seems to me, in
terms of our experiences or dispositions themselves, or on the
basis of bodily continuity. If we are not to follow them in this, and
not either to be committed to vacuity or give up altogether, how
can we proceed? How can we avoid the pit of some desperate and
wholly implausible description of what it is to be a self, and this
particular self, or the pit of total unintelligibility? To vary the
metaphor, we seem to be caught, or to have caught ourselves, in
an inescapable pincer movement. Is there in fact an escape?

I certainly think there is. The solution, it seems to me, lies in
the very special way in which each individual knows himself to be
the individual being he is and just what this is like. This is in no
way the same as our knowledge of the specific items about ourselves we have usually in mind when we speak of knowing who we
are. One obvious item of the latter sort is knowing one's name,
and other particulars such as may be found in a passport. Many
of these are items we easily forget, and it has not been unknown
for people to forget even their own name. But when I speak of a
special way in which everyone knows himself to be the person he
is, I am not thinking of such items. There is something more
basic, more persistent and unavoidable, than any knowledge of
my physical appearance, my history, my social status, my dispositions, likes and dislikes etc. These are all matters on which I
am usually the best authority, but it is the sort of knowledge
about me which others acquire in much the same way as I do
myself, and about which they may sometimes be more reliably
informed.

In short, I am not thinking of the sort of peculiarities by which
I would normally be described and identified, but of what it
means for all this, or for all that happens to me, and all I do, to
be happening to *me* or be done by me. Many things are happening to me now, I see many things and I am having these thoughts,
I have bodily sensations; and it could, not inappropriately, be
said that I am the person to whom all this is happening. But what
is it for it to be happening *to me*? The same things, or very nearly
the same, could be happening to other persons; they could look
out from the same window. Is the difference between them and

myself solely the slight variations in the experiences we undergo and the placing of these in a different setting from mine in the corpus of their experiences as a whole.

It seems certainly to be straining things to say that the only radical difference between me and other persons is that my experiences are associated with a particular body, or conditioned by it. The body is indeed normally of the greatest importance in determining what my experience will be like. The perspective in which I see things depends on the location of my body and other things appertaining to it, and I have stressed very much already our normal dependence on our bodies.[5] But if I am right in my earlier insistence that mental states are radically different in nature from physical ones, it would be odd, to say the least, to hold that the only sense in which I am the particular person I am has nothing to do with my status as a mental being. Nor is the concern or regard (or dislike) I may have for myself or others to be found mainly or directly in what our bodies are like. Bodily features have indeed a very important place in some of our affections, but they are so in close association with various properly mental attitudes. It would be perverse, or worse, to fall in love with a dummy, and even then, in most cases, as with children's dolls and bears, it would have been given some kind of personality beyond what it is physically. Even if it is maintained, implausibly to my view, that bodily continuity is a condition of personal identity, it can hardly be the meaning of it. We like or dislike people for qualities of mind, though not exclusively the severely intellectual ones, for the way they feel and respond etc.

But it is also implausible, though we shall return to that submission, to suppose that I am the particular person I am solely because of some pattern or continuity of my varied experiences, a continuity which, as we shall see, could well be extended in principle to the experiences of other persons; and the more explicit reason for maintaining this is that at any particular time I am aware of my experience as very distinctly and expressly mine regardless, or without any special thought, of how they came about or what may ensue a moment later. There is a peculiar immediacy, something expressly evident at the time, in the way in which I am certain that, in seeing the trees in the field, I myself am seeing them, it is me. There is no recognisable inferential movement here, not even the most subtle. I do not know what it would be like for it not to be me that is seeing the trees now, it is unavoidably an experience which I am having, however much others may have a like experience; and this is an assurance, whether made articulate or not, which affirms itself directly at the time in having any experience whatsoever. I just cannot conceive what it would be for it to be otherwise.

Take our stock example again — I am in pain. Can we give any meaning at all to a 'floating' pain, to there being the pain without its being the pain which I (or some other creature) have? Can there be just pain which is nobody's pain? This seems to me not just unlikely but inconceivable; and we certainly do not mean by this that a pain must be caused by some physical disorder. A pain (and not just a mental agony as distinct from a 'physical' one) may be induced by certain frames of mind. It need not be an imagined pain, whatever that would be. I could induce the sort of pain I have when my finger is cut by being predisposed to think that I am having it, or some similar factor — a tormentor could tie my hands behind and pretend to cut my finger. In some states at least a pain could be so induced without any damage to my finger. We can also certainly have pains without noting the physical cause of them — I touch the hot plate and only realise that it is hot from the burning sensation. It is not because my finger is swollen or cut that I judge that I am in pain. I know this the moment the pain begins, and there might be the swelling or wound which normally hurts without my being in pain at all. The pain is what is felt, it starts and lasts only as long as it is felt, although, as we have seen, we may find ourselves paying little heed to it, and thereby perhaps reducing or stopping it altogether.

But the pain is also invariably felt as *my* pain. I could not have it without its being *me* in pain. Nothing could be more ridiculous than to wonder whether it is after all a pain that I have. I am the one who feels it. In other instances I may indeed wonder who is in pain. A house has collapsed and someone is screaming within. I judge that someone is wounded and in pain, but I am not sure which of the inmates it is. This must often happen, and even when we note the wounds or the crushed limbs we may not at once be certain which of the victims are actually in pain at the moment and which numbed, even though conscious, into temporary insensibility. But if we are ourselves among the victims we are not in doubt at all as to whether we are actually in pain, or just have wounds that may begin to hurt at any moment. If we are in pain we do not, in our own case, wonder for a moment whether it is a pain that we have or someone else. We may be in doubt about the extent of our wounds and perhaps mistaken in supposing that we are wounded at all — I may not be certain in the dark whether the blood is oozing from my own leg or my neighbour's. But I cannot be in any doubt about my being in pain myself however brought about. To know this I dispense with all the evidence that would tell me how others fare. This pain is essentially a pain *I* feel.

The same goes for my thoughts, and all other experiences. Others may have similar thoughts, but I know without a shadow of doubt that the thoughts I try to express on paper now are thoughts which I am specifically having as a distinct experience. But, if I am also asked — 'What then is this "I" that has these thoughts and this pain, how is it in turn to be described over and above describing the thoughts or the pain, or noting them, what is the self or subject over and above there being the pain etc.?' — I am wholly nonplussed. There is nothing I can begin to say in reply, not because it is exceptionally difficult to give a correct description, but just because there is no description that can be offered. My distinctness, my being me, is quite unmistakable to me, there can be nothing of which I am more certain, but it is also unique and ultimate, not unique like a rare vase or painting where we can indicate the properties that make it unique, but unique in a simple final sense of just being itself.

I must repeat then that, just as we recognise the distinctness of mental processes which makes them radically different from physical ones, so each one recognises himself as the one distinct being that he is in the very fact of being so in any experience at all. I am aware of myself in being myself.

This may appear to be a particularly lame or tenuous conclusion. After all the fuss, I may seem to have said nothing about what it really means for a person to be the distinct person he is. I have simply said that everyone will know the answer to this question in his own case. Everyone will know who or what he is, in being the person he is, and there is no more that can be said.

I accept this, but I do not regard it as a stricture. There are many points, in our attempts to understand ourselves and the world around us, where we can only report what we find without further amplification or defence. As I have stressed already, we do not manufacture the world around us, or reason ourselves and the world into existence. We must take things as they are, and one of the points where we can simply indicate what is the case is the one about the exclusive, but wholly adequate, way in which every person is aware, in the way indicated, of the distinct being that he finds himself to be. Much turns, in philosophy, as I have also stressed, on our ability to recognise such points.

This was the line of my reply to Professor Bernard Williams when he complained[6] that talk about 'ultimates' means that a philosopher is 'running out of steam'. It is rather a case that at some point the steam is bound to run out, there is a limit to explanation. The same misgiving may, however, be put a little differently by stressing the seeming vacuity of what is being affirmed, and Professor Williams himself, along with Professor Flew and others, have often put their point in this way. An ethical intuition has a clear content, certain things are good or right, but nothing appears to have been said, in the account I have been giving, of just what it is to be a self beyond the alleged recognition of it by each one in his own case. This point was forcibly put by one of the gifted students in the graduate seminar I conducted for two quarters at Emory University in 1978. He wrote:

> In Lewis' theory . . . Each substantial self is thus *sui generis* and its being so is its unique and peculiar character. But just to be *sui generis* is a strange character indeed, for it is formal only and is lacking in any content connecting it with other such selves. What this implies is that substantial selves are logically indistinguishable except for being *sui generis*. Lewis is thus faced in his doctrine, I think, with the paradox of claiming that the difference between substantial selves is unintelligible but recognisable.[7]

Mr Metzler continues with a slightly different point:

> The strength of this objection may not be clear, for one may accept the charge but simply argue that it is a curious fact of experience as we find it. But for myself, I cannot see how other substantial selves could be recognised. For I have no direct experience of them as being somehow *sui generis*. It seems to be a merely logical feature, and accordingly the way it seems to me is that we are faced with the logical identity of indiscernibles.

Mr Metzler's perceptive statement gets very near the mark, but not quite. I certainly do maintain that the self is *sui generis*, but it is not thereby reduced to 'a merely logical feature'. I know myself as a unique existent. My being is not exhausted in being *sui generis*, but is *sui generis* because of what I know myself to be. This is only unintelligible in the sense that there is nothing I can say about myself beyond the affirmation that I am the person I find myself to be.

His second point concerns what we say about *other* persons. But that is another matter, and I hope it will be clear already that no one, on my view, can claim the same sort of knowledge of other persons as he has of himself. In claiming to know immediately that the pain is mine, because I am having it and cannot, I have been insisting, have it without being so aware, I rule out expressly the possibility of having the same sort of knowledge of another person's having a pain. It is only of myself that I can have the unique awareness in question. But I am entitled, and obliged it seems to me, in ascribing pain to others, to ascribe to them also the same awareness of themselves having it as I found to be essentially unavoidable in my own case.

Other persons are, in one sense, a radical mystery to me; I stress this, and I deem it of the utmost importance, as I shall be insisting again in the sequel to this volume, to recognise this. That does not preclude our having very full information about them in other ways, and live and intimate relations with them. I can have a very sound idea of the sort of pain you are in, and I must regard you, like myself, as a distinct individual having the pain. But what it is to be you, or any other, having the pain I cannot possibly know in the sense in which I have no problem in knowing what it is to be me having this pain. There is a barrier here, a limit to our encounters which we can never remove. But this itself involves regarding other persons as genuine distinct existences, in practice indiscernible at this level, but also, essentially and not just numerically, other. They are *sui generis* because of what they are in this way in themselves, and not just as 'a logical feature'; and it is for this reason, as we shall see again, that there can be no merging of persons such as many have thought possible and actually the case. The distinctness of persons is their distinct irreducible individuality.

This holds, however, for all sentient beings. There are differences of the utmost importance between us and brutes, but everything I have said hitherto, in this and preceding chapters, can be said, in strictly the same way, of sub-human creatures as of ourselves. Whether, for this reason, we speak of the 'soul' of a worm or an insect, or of one of the 'higher' animals, is mainly a matter of words. If 'soul' connotes moral or religious attainments, and the sort of destiny which this alone may be thought to make possible, then we could not ascribe it to creatures which have not the discernment to reach these and similar attainments. But I have not yet been concerned with such matter. I have been stressing merely the distinct nature of mental or experiential existence and the unavoidability, from what we know it is like to have experience, of there being some being or subject who has the experience.

This must apply to the dog or the worm as much as to ourselves. We cannot give a Rylean account of a dog in pain any more than we can of a man. It is not just a matter of observing pain-behaviour, or of counting on this on the basis of presumed regularities. We have every reason to conclude that the dog feels the pain as we do. It would also be absurd to suppose that the dog is aware of his pain because he observes how his foot is bleeding or hears himself yelping. The actual pain is the same for him as for us. But can we then think of it as anything other than a pain which one distinct individual has? It is not, any more than in our own case, merely the fact of there being the pain, or the mere connection of that with a particular neuro-physiological organism or body. It is not merely that the pain is due to the broken paw of this creature, or even, if that is the account we must give of it, somehow located there. It is a pain which this creature must feel, not something a body feels, but this live animal. We have to ask here, as in all cases, what it would be like for there to be a pain which was not individually felt. It seems to me just inconceivable, not because we are habituated to *talking* of pain as something which some creature has, but because it is impossible to think of pain or any sensation in any other way. Can we, we must ask again, make any sense of a mere pain or a 'floating pain'?

How far can we take this? How low in the scale of life and sentience can we go and still feel compelled to recognise some entity that has the experience? The answer seems to me clear — as low as there is any sentience. We have seen that this is itself a question of evidence. Just where does the behaviour we observe no longer suggest a response to some kind of sentience? What on this basis is the lowest or most elementary form of sentient life we have to recognise? Wherever it is, however fleeting and transitory, there we must also impute a subject of experience, however grandiloquent such terms may sound in their cases. How could there be any sensation that is not sensed by some individual being?

The issue may not be of importance at this level, but it is bound up with its counterpart at higher levels of existence, especially human life, where it has vital importance, as will be stressed in due course.

This is not, however, the whole story — not by any means. There are many other things to be noted before the picture is near complete, and these are not elusive, or quite as difficult to handle philosophically, as the very central theme with which we have been hitherto concerned. They include the way in which we may be said to be, not only the subjects of an experience as it occurs, but also an 'abiding' subject, the same in all our experience. There are also the ways in which, in a subsidiary but also most important sense, we may identify ourselves and be identified by description. Let us then turn to these matters.

4 The Self as Described — and Memory

There can be little doubt that we do identify ourselves all the time, both for ourselves and for others, by description. For normal purposes this is all that is required. This takes the same course, in essentials, as identification in the external world. We may indicate which table is in need of repair, or to be disposed of, by saying 'the round table' or 'the square table'. This will be in a context, this room or at least this house, where the description rules out any possibility of confusion. In the last resort we must have recourse to physical location. Two objects may be identical in all the respects of which we can think, two tables of exactly the same colour, shape, size, weight, the same material etc. There is no way in which we can say that one is different from the other. But one is in front of the window, one by the fire. If this were not the case, if there is no way in which one is different from the other, and they are in the same place exactly, then we have one table and not two. We do not always have explicit reference to spatial location in distinguishing physical objects. A vase may be unique if it is the only one of its kind actually made by a famous artist. It may also be the only one of its kind that I have ever seen, or the one that I bought. But we can at least conceive an exact replica of any physical object. Physical location would then be the only means of distinguishing the two, and even if it is not expressly invoked, it will figure in some way, the making of the vase by the artist in some particular place at some time, or the physical transactions involved in buying it, etc. But without going further into this particular issue, it is evident that we identify physical entities by some peculiarities which we can describe. They are distinct because of the sorts of things they are. They must have some distinguishing mark.

For normal purposes we identify persons also in the same way, according a central place to physical peculiarities. If I am alleged to have been at a certain place at some time, it will usually be because someone has seen me and knows what I look like or can provide a reasonably full description of me, or of some distinctive peculiarity of mine, to someone who is familiar with my appearance. This could be a vital part of evidence in a criminal case, especially if confirmed, should that seem necessary, in an identification parade. I am picked out by the person who claims to have seen me. My physical appearance is decisive. In serious matters, like a crime, attempts will be made to substantiate eye-witness reports of this kind by yet more reliable physical marks, such as finger prints. I am identified by some reliable means of identifying my body. This is also how we make persons known to one another — 'May I introduce Mr Brown', that is the person who is standing in front of us or whom I specify if need be by a glance in his direction. 'And which is Mr Smith?' — he is the person reading the paper in the corner.

We do not always, however, think expressly, much less exclusively, in physical terms. 'Who is Brown?' — 'Oh, he is the person who is always disrupting the meeting by asking preposterous questions, you will recognise him'. We may also be described in many ways, including physical peculiarities, for other purposes than identification. People want to know what we are like, not just who we are. Novelists present their characters in this way, sometimes directly and sometimes in the mirror of the opinion of one of the other characters — Mrs Bennet, so Jane Austen tells us, pronounced Mr Davey, on her first experience of him, as 'a most disagreeable, horrid man, not at all worth pleasing. So high and so conceited that there was no enduring him'. Some characterisations, in life or in fiction, are more reliable than others, not excluding the opinions we may form about ourselves. But whether they are sound or not in particular cases, there is nothing inherently unsound or improper in making such descriptions of ourselves or of one another. In applying for a post it is not out of place to give some indication of where my interests lie, and it is usual for others, in testimonials or references, to give some opinion of my character and attainments. What then are we doing in such cases? Who or what is being described?

It seems plain, if the main submissions I have been making hitherto are sound, that when we proffer descriptions of physical appearance or peculiarity, we are not strictly describing a person. Many writers of today question this, not only when they hold frankly corporealist views, but in other ways when, in accordance with what they take to be a philosophy of common sense, they think they can properly speak of strictly seeing a person's anger or pleasure or watch him enjoying himself smoking his pipe. Followers of Cook Wilson, as well as advocates of modern identity theories, are apt to think in these terms. But if I am right in all I have hitherto maintained about the radical difference of mental and physical processes, it must be insisted also that accounts of my appearance are just accounts of physical properties, however important these may be as indications of what the mental states are like. It is pleasing to be handsome, and awkward to be unprepossessing or lame or deformed or blind. But these, even the blindness as a physical peculiarity of my eyes etc., remain physical properties, however much they may affect my happiness or the course of my life, in its properly mental` form, in other ways. They may matter enormously for me, as other bodily features matter for me — my health for instance — but they are not strictly descriptions of me as a person, except for rough and ready purposes. It is not me that is tall or lame but my body.

It was said of a person once that 'his squint is mental'. But all that this meant was that the squint was in some ways symptomatic, or an indication, of an attitude of mind, possibly in some measure a cause of it. This is a matter on which I have said enough earlier, in *The Elusive Mind* and earlier in this book. Whatever we may say in 'ordinary language' or for day-to-day purposes, the 'wedge', in Professor Strawson's term, is inescapable for common sense and philosophy. But in that case, we must surely look for what appertains to persons as persons in accounts of properly mental properties of actual states of mind or character. We shall therefore leave strictly physical descriptions aside as not directly relevant to our present concerns.

There are two ways in which we may have descriptions of properly mental reality. One is when we give an account of what is occurring at a particular time, or what has occurred in the past, in the way of some mental event or experience. I may report that I am now thinking the thoughts which I try to put on paper, and that I am also glancing occasionally out of the window to look at the trees outside, or sipping a cup of tea etc.; half an hour ago I went out for a walk, last year on a certain date I went to a play. Although these involve physical activity, they are, in the first place, accounts of what my experience, including all I set myself to do, has been like. We ascribe similar experiences to others, just as they learn about mine from what I say or observation of me or other indications of what I have been doing. How we come to ascribe experience to others, since no one *has* any experience other than his own, is, as was noted, a matter of the proper explanation of what we observe. But in essentials, in what we report, the account we give of the course of our own experience is not substantially different from what we report of other persons. I learn that my neighbour has been thinking about philosophy too, or about his holiday or that he has been mowing the lawn. In all these cases we have been describing what in fact has been happening, though as mental descriptions they only include directly what our states of mind were like, including all we were setting ourselves to do and our perceptions and sensations.

In practice much of this description will include an account of physical processes as well. In almost everything we do, including severely intellectual activity, there will be the close involvement of mental processes with physical ones, as already stressed. Sometimes this will be more overt than at other times; when I go for a walk or play a game the physical involvement is very evident, but even if I am just puzzling something out 'in my head' and sitting (or standing) still, I at least maintain these bodily postures, and I may do much besides, like frowning or wrinkling my forehead — and all this involves physical processes of which I have no proper awareness, such as all that goes on in my brain. But, in the present context, all that concerns us is the description of various experiences or mental occurrences as such.

With this we may contrast the sharply different way in which we may describe ourselves (or others) in terms of how we are prone to react on various occasions. I may describe my likes and dislikes, my hobbies, my accomplishments and my failings, and so on. Instead of saying that I am thinking about philosophy at the moment, I may just say that I am a philosopher or interested in philosophy, that I am fond of swimming and am good at a certain stroke, that I am much attached to my friends but have no fondness for certain others, that I am kind or ill-tempered as the case may be (or others may say this about me). Mrs Bennet was describing how Mr Davey had actually behaved at the ball, but it could just as well, indeed it strongly inclines to become, a sketch of his character as it struck her. We can say a great deal in that vein about ourselves or others. We read people's characters or say what they are like.

The term in most common use here is 'disposition'. But we also use 'character' or 'nature'. We may be 'good-natured' or naturally kind. 'Character' is sometimes reserved for the more basic ingredients in our dispositional system, but it is also often used for the system of our dispositions as a whole. When we offer descriptions of persons in these terms, we are not describing anything they are actually doing or undergoing. If I am judged to be a very ill-tempered person, or known to be fond of swimming or a powerful swimmer, this does not mean that I am in a temper about anything at the moment, or that I am swimming now. It means only that I am easily put in a bad temper, that I take opportunities to swim when they offer and enjoy it, that I have a certain competence as a swimmer, and so on. These are accounts of general traits of character and skills or accomplishments; they say what I am prone to do or capable of doing, given the proper occasion and inducement.

We do not know anything about our skills and other dispositions directly, not even in one's own case. A man's character or nature is not something he can directly inspect, as we might examine a machine and discover, very fully in some cases, what it can do. An expert mechanic could judge with some nicety what the acceleration of a car will be, although he will wish to confirm his judgement by testing it. No one's character is open to him in this way, nor is it so to others. This was why those philosophers, like Professor Ryle, who gave an account of actual conduct and experience entirely in dispositional terms, denied that we have any private access to our own minds. We know nothing directly about dispositions and skills. We must go, in the first place, to what our actual experience is like, to what we actually find ourselves doing or undergoing in some way. Our bodies may indeed be examined, and much may be learnt in this way, in some respects, affecting the kind of experience we may have. An oculist may find the eyes of his patient to be quite healthy and be assured thus that he is in no danger of losing his sight. Another doctor may forecast protracted pain from some bodily ailment. Perhaps he would forecast also a state of tension and irritation. How far we can go in this way on the basis of advances in neuro-physiology is uncertain. For while much may be anticipated, on the basis of physiological evidence alone, about possible perceptions and sensations, once we pass beyond this, to matters like irritability and forbearance, many other factors are involved—the course of our thoughts and understanding shaping themselves largely, as was noted, by what is inherent in their own determination, affected in turn by training, education, individual influence and the influence of environment in more general ways. It seems inherently impossible, short of the complete identification of persons with their bodies, to have an exhaustive neuro-physiological science of character. In practice, we learn what sorts of persons we ourselves and others are by observing how we conduct ourselves and react on specific occasions.

We learn that someone is considerate, because we find him being considerate in a variety of situations, we learn of the fortitude of another by noting the way he bears himself in adversity or distress, we learn that someone is courageous or daring because he acts that way, and likewise we know by their deeds or frames of mind that persons are callous, timid, cowardly or cruel. They may not always behave cruelly or be cowards, but that is what they tend to be, and in describing them as such we ascribe a certain nature or character to them. That is what it means to have a certain character, and whether physiology helps or not, the main recourse is to what we can establish from particular observation. We have no other access to character.

The position here, as has often been noted, is akin to the way we learn the properties of physical things. We learn that the glass is brittle, not because we can inspect the brittleness as such, but because we have learnt in specific observation how glass of a certain composition is affected by blows or pressure. This may itself be explained by more basic scientific knowledge, we may deduce much from basic principles, but the principle is the same. We discover the way things are, not by inspecting general properties as such, but from specific instantiation. The parallel must not however be closely pressed at all points. For the relation between one trait of character and another will depend on affinities between the sorts of things they are as properties of conscious or at least sentient beings. The level of rationality will have much importance here, and this is why we generally expect one virtue to carry some others with it. There are relations inherent to what our dispositions are in themselves, although we can never be too rigid in such matters. Character is complicated, a normally courageous trait of character may fall before some particular kind of danger, and we may not always be able to count on the

kind-heartedness of a normally courageous person. Some characters are much more integrated than others, and all are affected
by particular circumstances in their development.

What is of most importance for us, in our present concern, is
that we are able to describe ourselves and others in the sense of
determining what our dispositions are like. This will extend to
natural aptitudes and acquired skills, and to the emotional states
we are likely to be in, as well as to the likes and dislikes, inclinations and aversions, which tend to lead more directly to action.
How reliable we are, in assessments of this sort, in our own case or
that of others, is a moot point. We are prone to much bias, and
there is much that escapes the casual observer. The expert, on the
other hand, may be caught upon some narrowness of his own
preoccupation or preconceptions. We rely extensively on writers
of fiction to be our guides in the vastly complicated world of the
play of characters on one another. But we all of us form rough
estimates of what we ourselves and others are like in the present
sense, sometimes presupposing some general things about the sort
of creatures we are and sometimes forming an estimate of some
particular person, perhaps in some specific regard, like his
capacity to be a teacher or an administrator.

There is hardly any need to stress the importance of the way we
recognise one another's natures and describe them to ourselves
and others. This is the very stuff of living. Whether we put our
thoughts in words or not, or articulate them in some other way,
we live in communities of persons who deal with one another on
the basis of what they take one another to be like. Without this
there could be no society but only chaos. Our understanding of
one another is imperfect, but without some reliable measure of it
we could do nothing together. In our closer relationships, the
impressions we have of one another are of profound importance.
We are loved or reviled on the basis of them. We have an ideal of
what we should be, or of what we would like to be. This need not
be understood in terms of a rigid type, as in Plato's *Republic*, but
we all have notions of what it would be best to be and the qualities
to cultivate and to avoid. On some views, most of all in religion, it
is thought that our existence has the purpose of our attaining, in
the 'vale of soul-making', to a distinctive refinement of mind and
character, but this may be achieved in simple unostentatious ways
as well as in conspicuous ones. At a more modest level, life would
lose most of its savour and enrichment were it not for varieties of

interests and attitudes which make up distinctive personalities.

There can be no doubt therefore that we require to know and to understand one another in distinctive ways, and so to ascribe traits of character to ourselves by which we are distinguished. But what sort of ascription is this? To whom or to what are our various peculiarities ascribed? In the corresponding case of the ascription of properties to external things, we may take one of two courses, either a realist insistence on objects altogether different from our own presentations but involved in the coherence or system they present, or some way in which the reality of objects is found in the pattern or system they present. The first way is ruled out where mental properties are concerned, for neither a causal argument nor a simple recourse to alleged common sense will give us any notion of what sort of entity it is that could be reflected in the patterns of either our actual mental processes or our dispositions. The analogy with properties of external things, as a realist sees them, yields no result here, which is perhaps why Kant was reluctant to think of the subject of experience as 'a thing in itself'. No schemata of mental properties points to a reality beyond them.

Can we then simply ascribe our dispositions to some system of our dispositions as a whole, finding no reality for them that is not in turn dispositional itself. This, I submit, is also out of the question. For dispositions, considered in themselves, have a singularly tenuous or shadowy existence. They are meaningless apart from the experiences in which they are embodied. They have no solidity of their own. But in all the particular experiences in which our dispositional traits are actualised there is, as we have seen, the essential awareness of the self which has the experience, and which is peculiarly involved with it as the experience distinctively its own, while at the same time being everything that it is in itself independently of having this particular experience. Everyone, it was urged, knows his own distinctively ultimate existence in this way. But if our dispositions have no significance apart from the experiences, or on-going mental events, they regulate, and if, in all actual experience, there is the further awareness of oneself, the descriptions which an account of our dispositions offer must surely be a description of the self which, in its basic distinctness, eludes all possible description. My dispositions are very much, indeed quite essentially, my own; it is for me to be proud or ashamed of them, but they so belong to me as

the person whom I also know at any time to be irreducibly
distinct.

We may bring this out in another way. Our dispositions
change. I may transfer my interest in one game to another, or
drop my interest in games altogether. I may become a kind-
hearted person after being spiteful and cruel, a religious person
after being wholly secular, or the reverse. I may become, as it is
sometimes put, 'a different person altogether'. But all this will
still have happened *to me*, I shall have changed *my* ways. Com-
pliments or reproach will be due to *me*, it is for me to feel elated,
or ashamed or remorseful. This means that I remain, in the most
basic sense, the same person before and after these changes.

Attempts have been made to account for these changes in
terms of affinities of structure and relation between earlier dispositional states and later ones; and I shall shortly be considering
some recent attempts to include all that matters in self-identity
under the cover of relations between the changes of our states of
mind or our dispositions. But for the moment I stay with the more
direct presentation of the picture as I see it, and what appears
crucial here is the awareness we have of ourselves as the unique
beings we are, if this is allowed, in having any experience. To
account for relations between states of mind or dispositional traits
without reckoning with so central an item as each one's initial
awareness of himself would appear to be a very quixotic torturing
of ourselves to solve a puzzle in disregard of the most obvious clue
that presents itself. We may exercise great ingenuity in the
process, but hardly that which conduces to philosophical insight
and understanding of the best kind.

For the same reasons we have to move very cautiously when
people speak of 'a pure self' and 'an empirical self'. There may be
no serious harm in this terminology, but it could lead us very
seriously astray if it led us to suppose that there actually are two
selves. There is only one self, known most explicitly as the subject
or agent in our on-going mental states, but it is the same self
which has the on-going state as peculiarly and essentially a state
of itself and has its dispositions, liable to change as they are, as
dispositions of the one being which each one knows himself to be.
To think of an 'empirical self' as some kind of adjunct to the 'pure
self', which I am essentially, would be to so detach my dispositional self from the self which I really am as to make it peculiarly
difficult to see how my dispositions could affect *my* states of mind

or conduct. We must not forget that they are only known in that determination.

We need not thus be daunted by seeming to be committed to the paradoxical view that, in one very obvious sense, any person may be described, by himself or others, and, in another more fundamental sense, may not be described at all. Philosophers have often found it their business to take the sting out of seemingly serious or fatal paradoxes, as when H. A. Prichard and W. D. Ross[1] maintained that in one sense a person may have acted rightly on some occasion, and in another sense not. They maintained that these two senses of acting rightly are quite compatible. In the same way, it is held here that we certainly can identify ourselves by description in ways that have great importance, for ourselves and for all who have to deal with us — we may be so described in terms of our physical appearance (or other bodily features), or of our particular history or of our characters and dispositions. But this in no way diminishes the force of insisting also that nothing specific can be said in the same way to indicate just what it means to say that this is a description of *me*, or that it fits me. The initial clue here is the awareness of himself that each one has in his own case — and on that basis ascribes to others in ascribing experience to them.

To consolidate this position, and to remove further possible sources of objection, we have, however, one further major hurdle to surmount. The self is known to itself, it has been urged, in the course of having any experience, however we delimit it. But how can we be certain that the self or subject which so presents itself at any particular time is the same as the self which we find in another experience? How do we establish our continued identity? In what sense am I the same person now as entered the room an hour ago, and was out having breakfast before that, and visiting some other town yesterday, and so throughout my life? How do we know, or what is involved in saying, that the pain I have now is had by the same person as had a like pain (or was at ease as it may be) yesterday. How are these two pains mine, but not the similar pain which my neighbour had yesterday. How do we bind our own experiences together, and thereby the dispositions they manifest, over a period of time as distinctly our own. Might not the self which has the experience at some particular time, and which is thus more than that particular occurrence itself, be

simply a phenomenon which manifests itself in each experience as
it happens?

The oddity of this supposition will be evident at once. But we
cannot leave the matter there. There are substantial considerations which may be firmly adduced in support of the continuous
identity which we all assume in practice and which cannot, in my
view, be conceived exhaustively in relational or structural terms.

Prominent among these are the considerations, already noted,
adduced by Kant and his followers. Our experiences are not
random; on the contrary we apprehend 'a world of objects', as has
been noted, which become intelligible to us and which we are
able in some ways, on the basis of our understanding of them, to
manipulate. This enables us to live in the world as we do. But, for
this to be possible, there has to be more than coherence and
system in the world which we do apprehend in this way, we must
ourselves transcend the fleeting momentary presentations of the
world or the flow of events as it proceeds, we must in some fashion
stand away from all this and hold it together in our thoughts in a
way that would not be possible if we did not live on ourselves, as
the same conscious subjects, from one phase to another. To
ascribe qualities to objects which are only partially disclosed in
our presentations at some time, as when the coloured surface is
seen in perspective and further deemed to be part of a desk sufficiently solid to hold our books and to lean our elbows on to
write, with other sides, weight and so on, to hear the footfall
outside as a footfall, all this requires the understanding of what is
presented now which is only possible when we make it meaningful
in the light of previous experience. But for that to work we must
be the same, in the previous experience on which we draw, as we
are now. How else could our past experience help us now?

The alternative would be that one experience, or even one
presentation, however we understand that, should communicate
something of itself directly to the next, as in some forms at least of
the theory of association of ideas, or of traces in the brain. These
suppositions, initially implausible as they are, have been so extensively criticised, in their traditional forms, that it would be idle
to go over that familiar ground again. I shall shortly, as I noted,
be looking at counterparts of the same suppositions in our own
philosophical scene. Here I will only note how strange and unfortunate it is that treatments of this theme, ranging from
Bradley's notable chapter I, book II, part II, volume I, of his *Logic*

to books and articles by H. J. Paton, A. C. Ewing and C. A. Campbell should, as it appears at least, be so little heeded today.

It has, however, already been intimated that the Kantian approach, in itself, is inadequate. A mere formal condition of experience, a logical pre-requisite, is not enough — least of all 'an imaginary focus'. It is also apt to set us on the perilous slope, so fatal to much idealist thinking, which leads to the ultimate elimination of 'finite centres' by absorption in the unity of the one whole or absolute. The self must be 'something', and I wish now to pursue the implications of all that has already been said on this score, and especially of the awareness that each one has of himself in the distinctness of his own being — I want to pursue this further, in supplementation of the strictly Kantian approach, by an expansion that relates specifically to the question of our continued identity.

To this end, recourse must be had to the way we may be said to remember. A distinction must be drawn between two ways in which we may remember. One is the way we retain some information or understanding we have acquired. I remember the multiplication table and how to add and subtract. In the same way I have remembrance of past events. I remember that it was King Alfred who fought the Danes, that the battle of Waterloo was in 1815, and a vast array, or a web perhaps we should say, of similar things. Most that we may be said to know or believe is of this kind. We have a vast 'storehouse' of such knowledge on which we may draw at will. But there is also a sense in which I do not remember any of the past events listed here. I do not remember King Alfred fighting the Danes, or the battle of Waterloo — I was not there. I remember that Plato was a philosopher, and I remember well much that he taught, and other things about him. How we justify this, and how far such remembrance is sound, does not concern us now. For, in a more fundamental sense with which we are to be concerned, I certainly do not remember Plato — he lived long before I was born.

We pass then to the strict sense of memory in which I may sensibly say that I remember having my breakfast a short while ago, having a car ride and picnic yesterday afternoon, and other events much earlier in my life. There is also much that I have forgotten in my life, although I know in other ways that it must have been. But there is much of which we say that we properly remember. Nor does this apply merely to episodes in my own life

— I may remember a boat-race which I watched, and which would certainly have mattered more to others, the participants especially, than to me; I may remember an accident in which someone was badly hurt. In this sense, what I have called the strict sense of remembering, I can only remember something in which I myself participated in some way, at least as an observer. However strong my grounds for believing that something happened — and perhaps very recently — I cannot say that I properly remember it, if there was no sense in which I was there. I may have been told what happened as near the event as makes no difference — a workman, repairing the roof of my house, falls off the ladder, and someone rushes in to tell me. I may give evidence in such a case, but I certainly could not truthfully say that I remember his falling — I did not properly witness that, I saw or heard nothing of it myself. What we strictly remember are the things which we ourselves undergo or observe.

In the cases when we do say that we strictly remember we seem to be harking back directly to the past event. This is not an easy matter to present. There can be no question of claiming that we actually bring back the past event. My eating my breakfast was over and done with half an hour ago. I do not literally live over this experience a second time when I remember it. However we may think of time, or play about with notions of a time machine etc., there is not the slightest requirement to suppose that we live through the past event anew every time we recall it, nor does it seem in the least likely, or even meaningful, to suppose that time is reversible in that way. All the same there is some 'recall' of the past event. I do not simply have strong reasons for believing that I had my breakfast half an hour earlier. There may be such reasons — the tray is still there, I am reasonably replete, I normally have breakfast before I settle down to work, the waiter collects my tray and is pleased with my saying how good the breakfast was, and so on. There may be any amount of evidence of this kind, but it is not on the score of that evidence, however irresistible, that I say that I *remember* eating my breakfast. I have no thought of evidence of any kind — I just remember.

This does not mean that I remember everything about eating my breakfast. There will be much to which I have not attended sufficiently for it to make more than a passing impact. Nor will I, in the normal course of things, remember eating my breakfast this morning for very long. Unless there is something very special about it, the memory will quickly fade. But as long as I do remember it, and when I actually summon up a remembrance of this and of other things past, there seems to be nothing in between. I can this morning recall at will the event of eating my breakfast, and the waiter coming in later for the tray. If I give evidence on the basis of it, this, in itself, will not require any corroboration, although in other ways corroboration may be valuable. But my own evidence is taken at its own value, just because I offer it as something I witnessed. If I am asked, 'How are you so certain that the waiter took the tray away'? I reply, 'Because I saw him', it is enough that I am certain that I saw him, and if pressed as to why I am so certain now, I can only answer, 'Because I distinctly remember it'. The memory is clear without intermediary. I do not look for evidence, because I remember it so well—it was very recent, and my recollection is firm and unclouded. I put every reliance on it, and others will take it as substantial testimony if they are assured of my integrity. Evidence of an eye-witness is usually exceptionally strong.

The strength and clarity of my recall of past events, especially recent ones, does not mean that my witness is in all respects impeccable and can never be questioned. I may, in the first place, have been mistaken at the time. I do indeed very clearly remember the waiter coming into the room, but perhaps it was someone else very cleverly disguised to impersonate him. As I am busy at work, and so just take a casual glance, I do not penetrate the disguise, and I may have no reason to suspect it. Detective stories rely much on deceptions of that sort. Mrs Miggs[2] gave very firm evidence that Plant (the suspect) was in his room at the critical period of the murder, she heard him poke the fire, just as he always did, answer the telephone and use his typewriter, she had seen him enter his study and leave it later. It seemingly presented an unbreakable alibi which foxed Inspector French till almost the last minute when the faintest of marks on the window suggested how the suspect may have left the room by a rope-ladder and let in a well coached impersonator. In spite of her clear memory, and her integrity as a person not open to any suspicion herself, her evidence was wrong when she insisted that Plant was in his room all evening.

Even so, it was not the recollection as such that was mistaken, the lady had heard the fire poked, the telephone answered, the familiar padding about the room. It was not her memory that had been tricked, but her understanding at the time of what was going on in the room above. It is possible also for someone to be tricked in this way, or to trick himself, after the event itself. It is always perplexing when eye-witnesses, of undoubted integrity, swear that they saw something from where they were standing which it can be proved in due course they could not possibly have seen from just where they were, there was some obstruction or the vital occurrence happened just beyond their vision round the corner. The delusion is a genuine one, and it could come about, possibly because at the time their imagination and their expectations on the basis of what they presumed to be happening filled in the gaps mistakenly in what they actually observed, or because they were sufficiently suggestible to honestly conclude that the denouement which the facts they did observe clearly portended, or the record as it became known later or other strong evidence, had in fact been what they had actually observed at the time.

But here again it is not the memory proper which is at fault. The deluded person has put a further interpretation on what he does in fact correctly remember. He has allowed his memory to play him false because he has allowed himself to read more into his proper recollection than is strictly there. Some persons, due to vivid imagination or their being very suggestible or strongly disposed to believe certain things, are more easily deluded in these ways than others. But it does not follow, even in these cases, that there is not a considerable element of genuinely recalling some aspects of a past event.

The issue, at this point, is apt to be unduly clouded by the fact that, for most persons, the recall of past events carries with it very lively and vivid images. I visualise the waiter collecting the tray, and if I have any doubt about it, I play the still familiar scene over in imagination and set my mind at rest at once — 'Yes, of course it happened, I can still very clearly see it all in my mind's eye, I have a vivid picture of his beaming smile when I complimented him'. Yet this vivid picture is not the memory. Perhaps I could never remember so well without the picture. But there are persons who disclaim having mental images at all, and even if this is due to faulty introspection, the seeming absence of much reliance on the picture confirms our view that the picture is not the vital factor. Vivid picture or no, what I am assured of when I have a firm recollection, most of all a recent one, is that such and such happened.

The picture or image is in any case only a slice of the total event, like a still from a film — the waiter standing at the door or holding the tray. But what we recollect is the total event in its complexity. The image is itself often incomplete, it varies and in time grows dim notwithstanding that our remembrance itself is still very vivid; 'like yesterday', we say of some distant event very clearly marked in our memories.

It does not follow that the memories proper are always sound or infallible. There is a hard problem about the fallibility of memory. Some try to settle this on strictly linguistic grounds — we can have no use for 'memory' they hold unless there are some reliable memories. This seems to me very unsatisfactory. We may decide to use the word 'memory' for cases where the possibility of error is ruled out, or where in fact there is no mistake. But this itself does not prove that in practice there must be some sound or genuine memories. As far as this goes all memory may be wrong. If that were indeed the case, the basis for most that we believe would crumble, for it seems that we have to depend on memory at some stage, our own or that of other persons, to establish any factual claim; and this itself is sometimes advanced as the proper validation of memory claims in general. That also seems to me questionable philosophically, and it seems also out of accord with the way we ourselves from day to day regard memory claims. We certainly do not trust our memories normally because memory claims have generally been found to be sound, and that is not because of the sophisticated reflection that this in itself presupposes memory, but because it is out of accord with the feel of having a memory of something. The memory state itself seems to exclude all doubt — as regards what is strictly remembered. I may be wrong in my view at the time of what was going on — as when I thought the impostor a genuine waiter. But that does not put the strict recollection itself at fault.

Are we then to conclude that our memories guarantee themselves? The disconcerting factor here is that there seem to be unmistakable cases of misremembering. Some of these seem a little less awkward than others, and we can perhaps cope with them with less strain on what we normally tend to think. Take the case of our seeming to remember some event in our childhood. I seem to remember being stung by a bee at a picnic when I was very little. But it may be that I have this impression because I have been told about it so often that there is a firm picture of it in my mind, and I take this to be a proper memory. That is not altogether surprising, for, as we have seen, images have an important role in the total process of remembering, and they could masquerade as memory proper. When the recollection is faint we may wonder whether we are not being imposed upon in this way by a mental picture which has grown out of many tellings of the event. When memories are more fresh we rule out this possibility. I have no reason to suspect that I am conflating my picture of the waiter with an unfounded recollection of his collecting the tray. The memory is very firm and clear.

And yet there seem to be cases of misremembering in mature normal experience. Absent-minded people not only forget very easily what they have done, or where they have put things, but think also they remember doing things they could not have done. I have mislaid my watch, let us say. I am also certain that I had it in the class this afternoon, 'I remember', I say, 'taking it out and putting it in front of me'. I conclude that I must have left it behind or lost it on the way home — 'I remember I had it', etc. But later in the evening I change my coat, and lo there is my watch. It was there all the time. When my wife comes in she tells me that she found my old coat lying around with my watch in it, and upbraids me for being so careless. I could not therefore have put the watch in front of me, and yet I seemed to have a firm impression of remembering putting down my watch on the table as the class began. In senility or forms of insanity this may become a common delusion. George IV, we are told, 'remembered' fighting in the battle of Waterloo. What account do we give of such cases, and how fatal are they to the notion that some memories at least guarantee themselves?

The explanation, in the case of my watch for example, would seem to be along these lines. Finding that I do not have my watch, I conclude somewhat rashly that I must have left it behind — I always carry it with me, so I must have had it in the class. This sparks off the picture of what normally happens, and that is so clear that I take it to be a firm recollection. Does this take the sting out of this and similar cases of misremembering? It seems to me that it does. My recollection of putting down my watch had certainly the normal feel of a proper recollection, that is what it seemed to me to be. But how could this come about, could there be a mistaking of the spurious for the genuine unless there were genuine cases, and these also the most common. That appears to me to be the answer, and, for the present at least, I shall take it as sound that, notwithstanding instances of misremembering, we do have, in most cases of seeming memory, a genuine calling to mind of a past event, or at least of our experience of it and the way it seemed to us, and that this normally guarantees itself.

What follows, then, for our main thesis, from there being reliable memories of the sort indicated? The main point is that when we do recall a past occasion we recall it in its fullness, not only as an occasion when something we remember happened but also as one in which we ourselves were involved; and this may be spelt out more explicitly by saying that *we not only recall what went on in the past but also recall it as including, on our own part, the same awareness of ourselves then as we have now*. I recall, if I may repeat this crucial point, having the same awareness of myself in the past occurrence as I have now of the distinct being I now find myself to be.

This seems to establish beyond the possibility of any dispute my continued identity in all the occasions in the past of which I have a firm recollection, and this can with every reasonableness be extended to the vast variety of cases of which I have every confidence of being able to summon up a remembrance if I turned my mind to it. This ensures my continued identity over considerable stretches of my life from early years. What, then of the rest? How can I build up, around the experiences which, through firm recollection, I can clearly ascribe to the self I am now, the other occasions of my life of which I have only indirect knowledge from the evidence available to all? This is the question to which I turn now.

5 Continuous Identity

There are extensive portions of my life, as it would normally be taken to be, of which I have no proper recollection, and which, in the normal course of things, I am never likely to be able to recall. There may be exceptional techniques, or drugs or some other device, by which a person may be induced to remember much of his life which he has otherwise quite forgotten. But I do not think we have to wait for anything of this sort to bring the occluded stretches of our lives within the ambit of my main concern at present. Let us then simply say, in the first place, that there is much of my life, as we would generally regard it, of which I have no proper remembrance. But I can be assured all the same of what must have happened in these forgotten interludes. This is because I can determine from independent evidence how things have gone for a person outwardly continuous with the person of whom, in various episodes, I have firm recollection and who must therefore, at those times, have been certainly me, the person I know myself to be.

It is in this sense, initially, that I will say such things as the following: I went to the local school from an early age, and later to a grammar school. The records will confirm this. Except for periods, fortunately few, of minor ailments, and the holidays, I was regularly at those schools from nine to four for several years. If one could lay hands on an old time-table of our lessons, we would learn that, on Tuesdays let us say, form four of the grammar school, in the year I was in it, had its Latin lesson from 11.15 a.m. to 12 noon. I can be confident that, unless it was one of the days on which I may have been ill, I was in the classroom for that form at the Latin lesson on any Tuesday during term in that year. But I do not remember any such occasion, and it is not to be expected that I would do so unless something out of the ordinary happened.

The most that I have is a general impression of what our Latin lessons were like, what the teacher was like, and the classroom.

'Oh yes', I might say, 'I remember old so and so very well, I can see him now'. This general impression is not without significance, for it is a remembrance; and how could I have acquired it, and a host of like impressions, if I had not been in the appropriate classes during those years? But none of this amounts to a firm re-collection of being in the class for the Latin lesson on a particular day. There are only very special episodes of my boyhood that I remember in that way.

We need not however be perturbed by these gaps. For in ad-dition to the over-all remembrances I have just noted, there is the easy dovetailing of all that I can independently establish about myself, from records etc., into the episodes of which there can be no question of my being the person involved. It is conceivable that, in the episodes and stretches of experience undergone by a person outwardly continuous with me and dovetailing into the events I remember, but no longer remembered by me, there was the obtrusion of some other subject or person, or a number of them. If such a substitution can be thought possible at all, it would be very strange indeed that it should coincide with the episodes I have forgotten, most of all when the boundaries of this are fluid and are variable according to interest or stress.

It could of course be argued that, in the episodes I have for-gotten, another subject was involved — and that this is the reason for my forgetting. But the passing of recent very complete remembrances, like my remembering in fairly full detail all I did yesterday, into dim or totally faded memories in a short while, very strongly suggests that this has also been the fate of much I lived through in the past which I am no longer, in our normal states, able to recall. In short, whatever may be strictly conceiv-able, we seem to be pushing philosophic doubt and scepticism beyond all reasonable limits if, once assured of my undoubted identity in the episodes I do remember from various periods of my life, I hesitate to build up around this all I can establish or assume about other events involving the same outward continuity. We are in fact home, as far as concerns the continued existence of the person I now know myself to be for the whole of the story that involves the same outward continuity — we are home in this way, as far as any reasonable misgiving is in question, the moment it is clear that I must have been the person I am now in all of which I have a proper remembrance.

If we should wish to give serious thought to the possibility, to which I have just alluded, that, at various stages or episodes of what would normally be taken to be the continuous life of one person, one subject or agent may be replaced by another, there would be the following additional difficulties.

In any particular stretch or episode of my life a great deal of my past is involved. Past experience much affects the way I view things now, not only in perception itself, but in the significance I attach to all that is passing. If I am speaking to someone who has called to see me, let us say about arrangements for a journey, all that has happened earlier about this project is involved; and likewise my attitude to my visitor himself is affected by what I have come to know about him, or about persons like him. These are only some of the more explicit ways in which my past affects the present. There is in fact a vast and subtle network of ways in which my past 'lives on' in the present determining the way I understand the present situation and my attitudes and reactions in it. This, moreover, happens extensively in the shaping of my attitudes by stretches of experience of which I have no explicit recollection. It would be remarkable if all this affected only particular stretches of what is outwardly one life while other past events shaped and determined the subsequent experience of another person, or a number of persons, alternating with me in what presents itself outwardly, and to myself as well, as a continuous story in spite of sharp changes of fortune and attitudes. The necessary dovetailing of the different lives into one another, in such a way that neither I myself nor those who observe me have the faintest hint of it, would be astonishing indeed.

It is worth recalling here how much of our understanding is shaped, not by exclusively physical conditions or determinants of experience, however important or indispensable these may be, but also by nuances and other inherent inter-relations of thoughts and experiences themselves, the way meaning determines meaning. This brings its own accentuation of the difficulties of the notion of alternating agents in what is outwardly a continuous story.

But there is a further considerable complication in the sustaining of our experiences, for most if not the whole of the time in our present existence, by physical or neuro-physiological conditions of great complexity in one highly integrated system. Could this be at the disposal of a number of quite distinct subjects? We can easily understand how a car can be shared by a number of persons. Now

I take it to do all I need and then hand it over to my wife or a friend, the hired car is driven today by one man, the next by another. But as the maligned Descartes himself insisted, we are not in our bodies like pilots in a vessel. The continued interaction is much more subtle and sustained than that. This is indeed the strength of the materialist case. I have argued that it does not require materialism or strict materialistic determination. All the same, the supposition that so peculiarly close and integrated a system as the brain and the whole of the neuro-physiology of one body could be alternately responsive to a number of distinct agents or even of just two, calls for assumptions which hardly begin to be plausible.

If we could isolate parts of the neuro-physiological system, or even some patterning of its functioning, so as to relegate one to the service of one agent, another to the other, we might find the suggestion tolerable, but that the peculiar intricacies of one such system as a whole should, as one whole which very extensively at least it must be notwithstanding that some parts are more directly involved in one functioning than another — that all this should be a vehicle for a number of distinct agents is hardly credible. The gaps and the variations would break the system. The intricacies which prompt my recollections and enter into my attitudes would overlap those of the twin 'possessor' of my body and block them at every point. Although we would occupy the body at different times, the effect would be like a computer being programmed in incompatible ways at the same time. Consider how a very slight damage to a brain can bring extensive paralysis of the whole system.

There would also be the peculiar problem of the lot or status of the twin occupant of my body when it fell to me to be 'in' it, and of mine when it was his turn. Does the subject who is not in residence cease to be for a period? This is not so inconceivable a possibility as might appear at first, as we shall see shortly when we consider dreamless sleep. Or does my twin, when he makes way for me, 'enter' some other body. How does it come about that vacancies are conveniently available just as required? Or does the absent occupant have recourse to some non-physical or *quasi* body, or subsist in a wholly bodiless state? Whichever possibility we favour, it is strange that most of us at least have no recollection, in the course of our normal embodied existence, of these incursions into a radically different situation. Perhaps this is not altogether surprising if such metamorphoses occur, for we certainly become very rapidly oblivious of most of our dreams — they usually fade the moment we are fully conscious. But we do remember some dreams, and it is difficult to believe that for much of the time we are leading some radically different existence of which in our normal embodied existence we have not the remotest hint.

For those reasons I do not think we can seriously entertain the idea of a number of different subjects or agents interacting with the same body in some sustained and continuous way which could make a seemingly continuous history in fact a series of interweaving dovetailing lives of a number of persons, outwardly one but in fact many. We may sum it up tersely, but not I hope dogmatically, by saying — one body one person; and if the arguments I have earlier advanced are correct, we may conclude that the person whose continued identity is most expressly established in cases of strict memory must also be credited with all the experiences and activities we associate with one continuous bodily existence.

This does not preclude there being occasional and limited interference with the neuro-physiological system of one person by another mind. Indeed, in one way, this is happening all the time. Other persons can determine what my brain states will be, or at least influence them, by placing me in a certain position, or obstructing my view; all communication involves interference of this kind. But it is possible to affect my brain state in other than the normal ways. A drug could be administered to me that would make me delirious, a doctor could operate on my brain and stimulate it in the process, as he might achieve a like result with electric currents. But in all these cases some other physical factor is involved. Could a mind have a more direct impact on the brain of another?

I do not see why this might not happen. It would clearly be paranormal. But the evidence strongly suggests that some paranormal events do happen. Telepathy might take the form in question, though it could also be understood to be a direct influence on the mind itself. If other minds, perhaps non-human ones or the spirits of the departed could, as is sometimes alleged, take over or possess our bodies, that might take the form of their being able, either deliberately or otherwise, to affect our brains in some paranormal way. If the possession of a medium during a

trance were not to be deemed a fraud or some purely psychological excitation of the medium himself, some welling up of
elements from a subdued sub-conscious, then it might not be unreasonable to conclude that, in the medium's ecstatic state, some
of the normal functioning of the brain and nervous system is
modified in the course of the paranormal impact of another mind
upon it. Mediums have been known to provide significant information which it does not appear likely that they could have obtained in the normal way. Clairvoyance might not cover all such
cases.

In that event, however, an explanation in terms of some direct
impact upon the brain — not the only possibility as we have seen
— would not at all amount to a proper take-over of the brain and
nervous system or the ousting of one occupant of the body to
make way for a rival. For a limited impact upon the brain, however startling, and one not of a long duration, would be very different from being totally responsive to that brain and receiving
stimulus from it in the way our normal experience is conditioned
by, and dependent upon, certain states of our brains and our
bodies generally. Even if it proved possible, as is sometimes envisaged in science fiction, to exercise considerable control over a
person by electrically affecting and controlling his brain, this
would still be 'one-way' business. It would not amount to a complete new embodiment. The difficulties in the way of the latter
seem to me so considerable as to rule out any but the most remote
and fanciful entertainment of it.

This relates closely to many 'problem cases' as they are sometimes called, for example the alleged interchange of personalities
in the same body, as in the celebrated case of Eve-White and Eve-
Black. The simplistic explanation here is that two distinct persons
took over the same body in turn and it was from this that the
subsequent film drew its main dramatic effect. But the facts do
not seem to call for nearly so drastic an explanation. It could be
just a less startling case of so-called 'dual personality', combined
with extensive loss of memory to occlude, in one personality, all
knowledge of the other, while retaining much other information
common to both states. It would still be a remarkable phenomenon, but not so remarkable or so fraught with radical difficulty as the more popular rough assumption. I have already
indicated what the latter difficulty would be — where, for
example, was Eve-White when Eve-Black was in occupation?

There seems little doubt that cases of dual or split personality occur. But what we must suppose here — and that is how experts proceed in handling such cases — is that it is the same person who is involved all the time, but with drastically different traits of character coming to the fore in the alternating states, together with total loss of memory in the one case of the occurrence of the other. It is indeed astonishing that there should be such complete loss of memory of very recent events, as would happen with the onset of the change. But we have a parallel familiar to all in dreams. We do remember and tell some dreams, but there is ample evidence that we dream a great deal more than we remember, and most people have the often frustrating experience of remembering a dream well for a very short interval of becoming awake only to lose it entirely the moment we are fully awake — or very soon after. Yet no one suggests that the person in the dream experience is other than the person awake later. In the same way in essentials it comes about, owing to special conditions, in which physical factors would have an exceptional place, and perhaps be the total explanation, that, in extreme cases of schizophrenia, one and the same individual passes from one state to the other with radically different traits of character involved — and extensive loss of memory. This is strange enough but the evidence does not usually call for anything more dramatic.

In schizophrenia, the person who suffers this is not aware — or at least not normally aware — of being identical with the person in the other state, simply because he is not aware at the time of there being another state. But his total unawareness of it does not preclude his being the same person in his role of Dr Jekyll as in that of Mr Hyde. We all undergo substantial changes of mood and inclination. In the abnormality considered here, the change would be much more extreme and involve an extraordinary loss of memory. This may be invoked, in extenuation of guilt or as a complete adequate excuse, more often than is warranted. But there do appear to be many genuine cases. But there is nothing in them to require the more startling and dramatic explanations sometimes offered of extreme instances. If memory were the essence of continued identity the case would be different, but I have invoked it merely as the firmest way of establishing our continued identity.

Other persons than the sufferer himself will of course know, if they can observe him in the alternating states, that the behaviour in both states is associated, or involves, the same body and, for the reasons already adduced, will be reluctant to admit any exception to the principle of one body one person without evidence which irresistibly calls for it. Some cases of schizophrenia are in any case not complete, and this also strongly suggests that the extreme cases are intensifications of conditions which neither require nor admit an explanation in terms of strictly distinct agents.

The position will be different, however, for those who adopt a different view of personal identity. If we think of identity in terms of patterns or continuities of experience — a view we shall note more closely in due course — there will not be the same finality about where we draw the line as to where one personality ends and another begins. But this in itself tends to cast doubt on the soundness of that theory, to the extent at least of its being rather far removed from what we are normally inclined to think.

If the question were pressed as to what sort of evidence would seem to establish that, in some cases of schizophrenia, a genuinely distinct person must be thought to 'take over', this would have, it seems to me, to be on the basis of some information exhibited by one of the alleged personalities which could not have been obtained by either of them in the normal course of things. If it could have been obtained by one of them in an earlier schizophrenic state, and thus in an existence presumably of the same person, this would not be enough. For we could still regard it as information obtained by one and the same person in an exceptional state. But if it could not have been acquired by either in the normal course of their common bodily existence, this suggests that one of them does lead a genuinely further existence in some form in the intervals of not being in this particular body. There could, however, be other explanations, in terms of telepathy or clairvoyance for example, notwithstanding that these would not seem to me to be initially as plausible as the more drastic explanation with all its additional perplexities. In the cases usually cited, there seems to be no indication of the exceptional information required.

A closely related phenomenon which is usually cited and discussed in contexts like the present one is that of very complete loss of memory. Tragic cases of this are known and again made the basis of dramatic fiction or films. The argument usually goes that a person in this distressing turn of events has no longer any notion who he is. He can tell you nothing about himself, not even his name or where he lives, who he used to be; he does not recognise his former friends or familiar places. He has lost his identity, we are apt to say, and there is obviously a sense in which this is true. But, in his unhappy state, the sufferer will know himself, in the full normal way, as the distinct person he is, and he will very probably, as has been noted already, bemoan the fact that 'this has happened to *me*'. If evidence becomes available which will establish his identity in the normal 'practical purposes' sense, both he himself and others will regard him as, in the strict and most literal sense identical with the person whose past becomes known in this way. He will be eager to know about his past, and the last thing he is likely to suppose is that his existence began at the point which his present memory reaches or when he 'lost his memory'.

In the sense with which we are primarily concerned, the phenomenon of loss of memory does nothing to upset the notion of the self as the distinct being which each one at the time knows himself to be and which can comfortably be thought to be continuous with the person presenting a bodily existence continuous with his present body.

Mention has already been made of dreams and their significance in this context. To those, like Professor Norman Malcolm, who hold that dreaming is not an on-going experience like waking consciousness, there is no help to be found here in the fact that we dream. But there has been so much severe criticism of Malcolm's view, including a lengthy discussion by me in chapter VI of *The Elusive Mind*, that I shall not open this issue again but simply proceed on the common assumption that dreams are an actual experience. In our dreams, I submit, we have exactly the same awareness of ourselves as the unique person that each finds himself to be as we have at all other times. But our actual physical body plays no direct part in this for the simple reason that I am not aware, in my dream (and most certainly not normally aware) of the disposition of my body at the time. If, when fast asleep in bed, I dream that I am playing tennis, I remain quite oblivious of my actual body curled up in bed. My actual body plays no part in the way I continue to think of myself as the person I am on other occasions. I just know myself to be *me* in the dream in precisely the same way as I do now writing these words. I shall likewise, in the dream, remember much about myself on other occasions and invoke much understanding of myself and my environment. This does not mean that the body is quite inoperative in the dream. Far from it. The way I dream will depend much on the state of my body, and especially my brain — in much the same way as in waking consciousness, that is, the brain state will condition the course of my dreaming without completely determining it; other more specifically mental factors, including associations, meanings, attitudes shaped by past experience, will come in also. We may thus fully allow for such familiar facts as the weight of clothes on the bed, over-eating, or a loud noise penetrating the dream state, affecting a dream. But I am not, in the dream, except in the twilight condition of slowly awakening or falling asleep, aware of the these factors. I fully take myself to be playing tennis, my opponent is for me a real person, not a dream person or image, I am quite convinced that I am hitting a real ball; and very rarely indeed, although there do seem to be cases of so-called 'vivid' dreams when people know they are dreaming, have we the slightest notion that we are dreaming or the faintest awareness of the actual state of the body curled up in bed.

In spite of this I have no more difficulty in identifying myself and thinking of myself in the normal way (in the dream) than I have in waking experience. In fact there is no radical difference in the experience itself. It is simply not as coherent or stable as waking experience and, like hallucinatory states, not related causally to the course of events in the physical world. If I dream that I am cutting down a tree in my garden, the tree is still there when I come out of my dream, and we say, 'It was just a dream'. But I did have an experience very similar to cutting down a tree, and some dreams have reasonable continuity and coherence within themselves — perhaps they have more than we think if we could remember them better. Within this experience I have precisely the same awareness of myself, as the person I always find myself to be, as in waking consciousness. If it seems, in the dream, that I am about to be hurt, if my hand is being thrust into the flame, I am frightened because of what seems about to happen to *me*. This will carry with it much remembrance of past experience, but that is not itself constitutive of what I understand myself to be as the distinct being that I am.

In my dream, I will have a dream body; I shall swing my arms to hit the tennis ball, or slip and perspire. But my consciousness of myself as myself has nothing to do with noting resemblances between my dream body and my real body or recognising myself bodily. Normally, in dreams we are too much absorbed in the total passing scene to note our own bodies, and if we did and found some sharp discrepancy, if the lame dreamt that he was healed, there would be no question of wondering who he was, but surprise and, in this case joy, at finding himself so much changed physically. The change would be of *his* seeming bodily state.

Our consideration of dreams brings us to a further problem which many critics will consider a very serious one for a Cartesian. What would the situation be if we lapsed into totally dreamless sleep? Whether this ever happens is not so easy to settle, for the absence of the eye movements by which a dreaming state is taken to be most unmistakably indicated might not strictly imply that there was no dreaming at all — it might merely mean that there were some dream states which did not reflect themselves in this overt physical condition. Plato seems to have thought that the more soundly we slept the more alert our minds would be. But be that as it may, we cannot rule out the possibility, improbable though it seems to me, that we sometimes fall, when asleep or in some like state of unconsciousness, into a totally dreamless state, in which we have no experience of any sort, however faint. If this comes about what do we say about the self? Does it at least persist?

There are many doctrines of a 'pure self' which find no difficulty here. The aim of some religious disciplines seems to be just to detach the self as completely as possible from all outward existence, to withdraw into pure consciousness. This paves the way also, in many forms of mystical monism, for the identification of all selves with one another or their absorption into the one Supreme Self. In a recent study, Professor W. T. Stace commends just this view.[1] For my own part I have never been able to make much of this position, quite apart from its wider metaphysical implications. Just what would it be like to simply exist as a subject having no sort of content of experience whatsoever, sensing nothing, imaging nothing, thinking nothing, intending nothing, a state of consciousness directed to nothing whatsoever? According to some thinkers this is a highly rarefied and most precious state of being, but for my own part I find it difficult even to conceive of it or make it meaningful, much less attach the highest worth to it.

To be relieved of some preoccupations which may be obsessive or too dominant, to break away as a discipline from limiting concerns and cultivate greater detachment, this may be very fine, at least as an occasional discipline. But what it would be like, not merely to be deprived of all external stimulus or perception, but of any similitude of these *and* of all content of thought in any form whatsoever, to be suspended as pure being in a total void, emptied even of all private cogitation of any form or its like, of that I can form no conception at all. When I attended, mainly as an observer, a short meditation course in Japan under the expert guidance of Professor Masao Abe, the advice constantly given to me by my mentor was — 'Stop thinking'. But in this I never began to succeed, although I could well understand what it would normally mean to leave aside my usual ways of thinking. To stop thinking in every sense, not even think about not thinking, to make one's mind a total blank, this seems to me, not just exceptionally difficult and far beyond the reach of a novice not extensively committed to arduous disciplines, but inherently impossible. I fully allow for all that is said in these contexts for the emptiness which is also fullness, and shall return to the wider aspects of the subject as a major concern elsewhere. But taken in its strictest, most literal sense, I must confess that I can make nothing of the notion of a totally empty consciousness, a mind that is not minding anything whatsoever, pure rarefied being, the self and nothing but self.

In that case, what of dreamless sleep? The proper answer, it seems to me, is that, in the event of strictly dreamless sleep, we simply cease to be. Is that disconcerting? In no way it seems to me, though many will find it so. Have we then been dead for some period? This is largely a matter of words. The body will certainly have continued to function in the normal way, and the health of the body will not have been impaired in any way — or, if that is not the case a state of dreamless sleep will not be something that happens in the case of normal sleep; we would know that something untoward had happened, and might be able to connect it with such evidence as we have of a probably dreamless state. That is not our normal supposition. When we entertain the idea of dreamless sleep we assume it to be a state into which we have lapsed without any consequent malfunction or any normally observable indication of it, much less anything catastrophic. Our lives resume their courses in the normal way without any consequence we should especially deplore.

The most that we seem to have missed, in that case, is a few

minutes of dreaming existence which would in any case be presumably a very low grade of dreaming consciousness on the
borders of a blank unconsciousness. Even if many minutes are
involved, that would not seem to deprive us of anything we would
particularly value or which could have a place of any importance
in the serious concerns of our lives. What do we miss, then, if, in
supposedly dreamless sleep, we simply pass out of existence for a
period, provided that everything afterwards assumes its normal
course — we begin to dream again and later wake up with our
normal memories and faculties unimpaired? Practically nothing
would have happened to cause us alarm or distress.

But, it will be said, the real difficulty arises at the theoretical or
conceptual level. If a person is the subject or agent and not itself
in any sense corporeal, we must be pronounced dead on the
present assumptions in dreamless sleep, whatever may be appropriate to say for clinical purposes. I should not myself seriously
object to its being put in that way, but it would I fear be apt to be
misleading, as we associate death with a finality of physiological
functioning not compatible with the normal resumption of
awareness and conduct in this life. If death merely means missing
out on some minutes of low-grade awareness, then it is not disconcerting to suppose that we have been dead for a period during
which the conditions of our revival and continued existence were
maintained. Some might still worry about the prospect if they
understood it, but it would be an unreasonable fear. Indeed, if
sleeping and dreaming were very rare occurrences, most of us
might feel some nervousness in being told we were about to
undergo them. The main point is that everything is as it was
before in the event of a period of dreamless sleep. But is it — if
that involves a period of non-existence? Can this be bridged on
the submissions I have been making?

This is where the conceptual difficulty will be pressed. How can
personal identity be maintained across a gap which involves the
total suspension or annulment of the subject. I fail however to see
any genuine difficulty here. Admittedly the position would
appear simpler if we thought of our identity in terms of some
continuities of experience and attitudes, in the view to which I
shall return. But in what sense does a distinct and ultimate entity
maintain its identity beyond periods when it totally ceases to be?
This point may be pressed, but I confess that I find no serious
difficulty in it. I know myself at any time as the person I find

myself to be, and I know, from strict memories and other supplementary ways as indicated already, that I am the same as the person who had other experiences in the past which I describe as my life. I *do not know*, in the last analysis, how this comes about or is possible, except in the sense of knowing the physiological conditions on which it depends in our present existence. I just find that, in certain conditions, which may or may not be dispensable in some other existence, that my own being is in fact continued, at least over extensive periods and, as we have good reason to believe, for most at least that would be regarded as my life. This may be just something we find to be the case; or we may look for further reasons for it such as our being maintained in existence by a superior being or a creator god. Those are further questions which may be handled in various ways, from secular or pious agnosticism to firm theistic belief. But they do not concern us at present. All that matters now is that, in some way of which we can give no explicit account ourselves, we do find ourselves, as distinct entities, maintained in existence from one moment to the next.

In that case, there is nothing peculiarly bewildering in the supposition that the identity of the self is maintained beyond a period of its total suspension, if that ever happens. I find myself now to be the person I was half an hour ago, but I have no notion how this is possible, in the last resort. The position would be no different if I found myself continuing to exist in the same way after what I had reason to believe, or to suspect, had been a period of total non-existence. I would have my normal awareness of being the person I am and I would have my recollections of my previous states which I have the normal reasons to trust and which make a coherent continuous experience. There is nothing in my knowledge of myself to make this inherently inevitable, but where, in any case, do we find such inevitability in the world around us? We certainly do not sustain ourselves in being, except in the sense, here irrelevant, of attending to the healthy condition of our bodies on which we find our present existence to depend. Our being the persons we are, after a possible period of annulment or suspension of being, and of our having ways of being aware of this, is no more remarkable, in the last resort, and no more amenable to an explanation explicitly within our own grasp, than the fact of our existence in any respect whatever.

This is also the context in which general considerations about the nature of substance are apt to be raised, it being thought that, if continuity of being is to be maintained, especially over periods when all activity is latent or potential, there must be some substantial structure, or substance in some other form, to maintain these potentialities. For my own part I have little notion what a substance in any of these senses would be, any more than I can understand the alleged under-pinning of our perceptual experience by the supposition of a 'something I know not what' altogether different from all the presentation of the world around us as we actually find it. The coherence of perceptions is sometimes thought to require a realist view in the sense of some physical reality altogether different from what is actually presented, but I have never understood what explanatory functions such postulations might be thought to have — Berkeley, in my view dispensed with them finally. Much less have I any notion what the self, as substance, could possibly be, or what the postulation of it serves, beyond the recognition of the self as the particular continuing entity which each of us finds himself to be. How, in the last resort, such entities come to be sustained, beyond noting the physical conditions they have, is a matter beyond explanation or direct speculation by us.

Another phenomenon which deserves to be noticed here is that of alleged 'out of the body' experiences. Claims to have had such experiences are very common in some cultures, but in a form which is peculiarly difficult to assess, or indeed to apprehend properly. The most tractable form of this claim is that which is sometimes made by patients who have been under anaesthetic for surgical treatment. Being under anaesthetic they would be quite unaware in any normal way of what was going on in the room. There would be no normal stimulation of their senses, they would see and hear nothing. Yet some have been able to describe what went on in very specific ways during the operation, observing it, so they aver, from a point of view on the ceiling or as if they were suspended from the ceiling or peeping through it. They have indeed 'seen' what happened in ways that would not be in their line of vision flat on the table. These claims go far beyond what an imaginative person with some knowledge of operations might have fabricated, or any dream he may have had. They have detail and accuracy which takes them out of the range of normal explanation.

There are however various explanations which might be offered. The patient might have got his information telepathically from others in the room, either during the operation or immediately after it. On the whole this seems to me less likely than that the patient was able to witness the actual scene in some fashion as he describes. It is hard to find an explanation that fits the facts better, and where there are genuine witnesses to confirm the reports, one is strongly inclined to accept the explanation at its face value. This makes one more sympathetic to wilder claims which do not admit any proper verification but which seem to be made in all sincerity and which purport to describe reasonably common occurrences in some cultures.

In India I have frequently spoken to persons who claim to pass out of their bodies quite frequently and without the stress of unusual circumstances like an operation. It is hard in such cases to suppose that the narrator is simply under a delusion, he has not been dreaming but purports to describe what others can vouch for in the normal way. Credulous they may be, and large allowances must be made for that, but they are not repeating what they have on report from others. Nor are they just pulling our legs or setting out to impress us at all costs. Some are highly intelligent and learned persons, and one is little inclined to suspect them of downright dishonesty. All the same, the oddity of what is maintained, often deepens one's suspicion of its genuineness, however honestly intended.[2]

Some, indeed, describe the process of exiting from their bodies in very literal terms, as if they were literally leaving one frame and location to function in another, like a snake leaving its skin, except that it does not resume it later. Much of this is bound up with the notion of our having various bodies all the time, unknown to ourselves or to most of us, a gross body and an ethereal one. This raises questions into which I will not enter here. I will only say that my natural scepticism is hardened when I listen to ready accounts of leaving the body through the top of one's head as if it were not peculiar at all — why the top of one's head, and what does this mean, except as a feature of early mythology? I can take more readily the notion that one simply finds oneself having experiences, from a point of view other than our bodily one, of what can be normally observed of the world around us — and sometimes, allegedly, of a quite different but fully real world.

The important question for our purpose is — suppose it be

allowed that some alleged cases of 'out of the body' experiences are genuine, what, in relation to the main themes of these chapters should we say about them? In the first place, it would seem clear that it is possible to have some observation of our physical environment without the usual stimulation of our sense organs and the consequent neuro-physiological changes, culminating in a brain change. The patient under anaesthetic on the operation table would not have perceived the nurse drop something and pick it up, but neither did he dream it; in some sense, *quasi*-perceptual and dependable, he *saw* her and *heard* what the doctor or theatre sister said to her — how otherwise could he describe and remember it? If this, as is averred, does happen, then it is most intriguing and significant. It means that it is possible to have an awareness of the world around us, in most respects the same as in perception, including perspective and a point of view, independently of normal neuro-physiological processes. There is thus opened up a possibility of a mode of existence and of apprehending to which we do not often give serious thought and which most contemporary philosophers are committed to repudiate from the start.

How much does this involve? Does the patient, when he sees things as from the ceiling, have some kind of *quasi*-body, as we have in dreams? If so, is there anything in it, as there is not in the dream-body, corresponding to the neuro-physiological system? Has it a brain? The very strong presumption here is that there is not. The body, if there is more than a point of view, serves a psychological purpose. It does not have organs that are actually stimulated by waves of light etc. What then of the actual physical body on the table. We cannot suppose that the patient sees and hears because his real eyes and ears are stimulated — the anaesthetic has seen to that. Are the body and brain involved in some other way as they certainly are in dreams. This is certainly not precluded by the patient being 'out of the body', for although he has a locatable point of view, and perhaps some kind of body, the mind itself, as I have especially insisted, is not in space or spatially related to the body. This, by our main contention, is no requirement of the conditioning of mental processes by bodily ones. There is nothing in principle to prevent the brain being involved. At the same time the odds seem heavily against that, for it is not the wild and random experiences of dreams that we have but the apprehension of events in the world around us, as observed by others as well, which normally only involve the brain through stimulation of sense organs relayed to it. The very strong presumption is that the actual brain and body are not involved in any way in genuine 'out of the body' experience, especially (or perhaps we should say more obviously certain) when it is also an experience of the world around us as perceived by others. The possibility thus opened out is a novel and exciting one — and incidentally one which should give the out-and-out materialist much to think about, though it is not in these exceptional cases that the main chinks in his armour are to be found.

Does this relate also to questions of self-identity? It certainly does. For the person — the patient in our example — who has the 'out of the body' experience will undoubtedly report it as an experience *he* has had. He does not doubt that it is so himself any more than others of us do in dreams. He will report what he has 'seen' or 'heard', and here we have, therefore, a sense of one's own identity, taken to be similar in all respects to our normal awareness of our selves, but in which the actual physical body is even less involved than in dreams. Whether such a person, in the course of this experience has some kind of body, for which a dream body would presumably be our model, or simply 'sees' things from a point of view or perspective similar to that of normal perception, he is able to observe, as an experience as much his own as normal waking consciousness, the scene to which others in the theatre also bear witness. It has been thought that, in the absence of our usual somatic sensations, we would lose the sense of our identity. This seems clearly belied if 'out of the body' experiences occur in the way described. It seems unlikely that, even if the patient is aware of having some body as in dreams, he will also have somatic sensations, and if he has, they are highly unlikely to be those he would have as directly occasioned by the state of his body. Total sensory deprivation, we are told, would lead to a total dissolution of one's sense of identity. We do not have such total deprivation, in all respects, in the cases considered. For the patient does 'see' and 'hear' in some way. But we are certainly approaching a state of the absence of all which our actual physical body sustains.

The facts, as we have supposed them to be, would, of course, be consistent with an account of our awareness of our own identity in other terms, for example some continuity of experience, if such an account commended itself in respect to normal experience. But if the account, as offered in these pages, is sound, we must assume, in the absence of any indication that self-awareness is different in 'out of the body' experience — and how could it be when the patient reports what *he* 'saw' while under anaesthetic etc.? — that in these cases of at least greater independence of the bodily state than normal, almost total independence of it, the sense of one's distinct identity remains and memory reports of the experience have nothing to distinguish them radically from the sort of memories we normally have. This has much relevance to questions of identity in a possible future existence.

The reference which I was making a short while ago to substance brings me to an objection to my general thesis to which I am often thought to be very open. I am not much attracted to a severely realist view of the external world, favouring (as indicated) more a somewhat Berkeleyan form of phenomenalism, not, as will be very evident, in the sense which Berkeley also would be most concerned to reject, namely that we and the world around us can be wholly understood in terms of the flow of our experiences. Indeed, like Berkeley also, I not only insist on a genuine self that is known independently of what the particular course of my experience discloses, but that also, in our presentations in perception, we are confronted by what is over-against us, not ourselves or states of our own minds. The coloured surface is certainly not a state of my mind, whatever we say of the smell or the hardness in the resistance to touch. There is, I maintain, a world of nature which is not me. At the same time I find it difficult to conceive what this can be that is not dependent on the way it is presented in experience. It is not my perceiving, but can any of it properly exist when not perceived?

When I look out on the field outside my window, my state of mind is not green. I apprehend the greenness but could this particular green expanse, with just the shade I apprehend at this very moment, exist except as perceived by me? If it does what of all the slightly different shades and shapes which others see and which I have seen during intervals of looking out on the same scene? Are all these independent and abiding? If we start to think that way we are in no time on the slope that leads to naive realism. Can anyone go along with that today, now that the implications of it have been made very clear? Bertrand Russell could at one stage in his career, but not for long. But short of supposing that an end-less number of hues and shapes which might be presented to our senses in all varieties of conditions literally exist all the time, now some being disclosed, now others, we must, if we adhere to a strictly realist view of the external world, present it as some kind of further structure which we invoke or postulate to account for all that is presented to our senses, but of which nothing is known in other ways.

But nothing seems to be gained for our understanding of the world in this way. I have little love of the principle of parsimony in itself. The simpler explanation should not be perferred just because it is simpler. We must account for all that we find to be the case. But we have no contact with any alleged physical reality in any more direct way than as an explanation of what comes to us in our presentations, and the supposition of there being that reality, as some quite distinct existence, seems to add nothing to what can be fully accounted for in terms of the irresistibility and marvellous coherence of all our presentations. This, from the point of view of common sense, makes the world around us very odd in some respects, but it is bound to be that in any case, and philosophers must follow the wind of the argument wherever it takes them. Is there any point in postulating something, short of transcendence itself, of whose nature we have not the faintest notion and which affords us no explanation of the facts which is not already available to us?

It is sometimes thought that we do have, in basic scientific concepts, some notion of what the constituents of a realist physical world would be. But this just begs the issue, for what are these non-observable physical entities which are not compounded out of the amazing intricacies of the way things happen, and can be anticipated, in the world as it is in fact presented? The case of our non-observable mental processes and our own identity is quite different. For here, I have maintained, we do have immediate apprehension, in one's own case, of these realities on their own account and not as explanatory principles. They are also given, and we know how we think of them, however little there is to say. There is nothing corresponding to this in the notion of pyhsical entities somehow supporting the world as we actually find it.

The only recourse, it seems to me, that the realist can have here is to the appeal to ordinary language and the frame of mind of Dr Johnson. But this has been very much blown upon now, and the effect of it appears to be to give up philosophical thinking altogether — there are tables and chairs, we all know it and there is an end of it. But we do not in fact know any of these things in the sense the realist has in mind. We only suppose it to account for other things.

There are problems for the realist also about space. For the actual extended surfaces that present themselves to us, according to our perspective etc., must oust one another in the competition for location in any space that is strictly continuous with the private Space in which they are actually presented to each of us. This is a much more substantial and intriguing problem than is generally realised by students of perception. I have myself tried to bring it more to the notice of philosophers.[3] If I am right there is a radical privacy about Space also as it figures directly in all our experience, notwithstanding that we construct out of our private Space the public Space of common sense and science.

If all this is sound, then, it is urged, the main thesis of the preceding chapters is open to a very serious objection, namely that I am not defending, as I claim, a properly dualistic view. I am not much concerned about the appropriate label. But more than that is involved. The argument is that, in the light of the views which I have just outlined, there is no proper recognition of a distinct, independent material reality to be contrasted with the mental reality of states of mind and persons. I see the point of this objection but am not much daunted by it. For I have insisted especially that, whatever the complexities of perceptual experience lead us to think, the world that is presented to us there is in no way mental itself. My state of mind is not green when I view the field, or the green patch, I observe when I look out of my window. The world of nature is over-against me, I encounter it, and in whatever sense it may be said to be also mind-dependent I certainly do not make it, it has its own laws, as discovered by the scientist, and we do not set those up ourselves. If a skull were opened and I looked within I should certainly not be looking at thoughts, but at extended matter. Meaning and the laws of thought are quite different from extended things.

In short, the question of the nature or status of the external world is a quite distinct further question which has no immediate bearing on the main views I have been advancing. Whether one inclines to a realist view of the external world, and in what form, or has sympathy with some kind of phenomenalism, as regards the status of matter, the contrast between mental existence and the external world, as encountered in perception, remains a radical one for which the vindication must be found in what we find mental existence to be like in our own experience. It is not merely that external things are extended, but that they are apprehended as essentially of a different order from the thoughts or sensations or other constituents of our minds.

The idea has also been mooted, though not very often in Western thought, that the self which 'has' the experiences may be of some still further different order from the mental states themselves. There would be more to be said for this, in my view, if the self were simply posited to explain the kind of experience we have or regarded as some 'thing in itself' altogether outside the range of our awareness, a mysterious something 'beyond' which we have to invoke. But it seems evident to me that this is not the case. We know the self, in essentials, I have maintained, better than anything else, however impossible it may be to describe it in the basic sense in which everyone is the person he is. But, I submit, the affinity of the self or subject, as known in the way indicated, with the experiences it has is very close — and I have stressed this more than once. I am myself in having my experiences, and I do not know how we could begin to think of the 'self', as known in this way, in any other way than as essentially of the same order of being as the mental reality of the states of mind we contrast, in the most basic division we know, with material things.

A further misgiving, which some appear to have, concerns the seeming static and unchanging character of the self, as presented here. Does the self not develop, it will be asked? I am not quite sure what is the real worry here. There is obviously a very important sense in which we all develop, and may regress also, as in acute senility. I have skills and aptitudes now which I did not have as a baby or as a little boy. All the same, this is a change that has come about *in me*, I am the one who has acquired these further skills. That the self, as such, is a constant factor in these changes is in no way detrimental to their importance. On the contrary, I am proud or ashamed of the way I have developed just because it is myself to whom it has happened. But the me that is involved here has not itself changed, I am strictly the same person as I was as a baby, and I do not see how this can properly be admitted without insisting that in all changes of states of mind or dispositions there is something that remains unchanging. That this has no obvious function in the changes being the kind they are does not detract from its importance; on the contrary how could the changes matter in the way they do except as changes which one and the same person has undergone.

The root difficulty here, as in so many contexts, is that the model we are disposed to adopt comes so much from our thought about external things. We picture some kind of inert, functionless quasi-tangible entity persisting through all changes of states and attitude. But this is just where we should most avoid models taken from external reality and consider the self as we find it, sensitive, dynamic, the very core of our living being, and also very peculiarly involved in having the particular experiences and dispositions it does have, as has been very specially stressed earlier.

I see no reason therefore to abandon or modify the view that, at the core of our existence and experience, there is an abiding entity, what each of us essentially is which remains what it is, myself in the strictest sense, through all changes of fortune or character and which will persist through even more radical changes of circumstance and status than we encounter in the normal course of our present lives. But in the last reflection we are getting on to another issue. For the moment we must turn to consider more explicitly than hitherto some of the alternatives to the view of self-identity I have advanced, and especially the contention, for which there is powerful support in recent philosophical writing, that continuity of experience, rather than strict identity, is the vital consideration. This is what will occupy us next.

6 Identity and Continuity of Experience

I would like to begin here with a celebrated article by Mr Derek Parfit which has, understandably, been the catalyst for a spate of very lively recent discussions. It is entitled 'Personal Identity' and was published in the *Philosophical Review* 1971. Professor Penelhum claimed[1] that this work 'has largely transformed the discussion of self-identity in the last few years.'

In one respect I find Parfit's position a little obscure, in spite of the delightful clarity of his writing. His central theme is that the notion of identity does not have the importance normally ascribed to it in the concerns we have usually in mind, questions of survival or moral responsibility for example, when we give special philosophical attention to it. All that matters, for the concerns in question, is perfectly well assured in a proper understanding of the continuity and connectedness of experience. It is to these matters, therefore, that we should turn. We can forget about self-identity in the strict sense, for 'all that interests us — all that matters' is provided for in some aspect of the continuity of experience.

The point which is not altogether clear to me is what, after all, we do say, on Parfit's view about personal identity. He is not, in what he proceeds to say, giving an account of such identity in terms of continuity of experience etc. Indeed it seems clear that he regards identity — 'a one-one relation' in his terms — to be certainly different from the relations he has in mind in what he tells us about continuity of experience. 'Identity is all-or-nothing. Most of the relations which matter in survival are, in fact, relations of degree.[2] Parfit is not, therefore, offering a reductionist alternative to the sort of view of identity I have been defending. But does he have any view at all about it? I suspect he would not agree with my view. But can he, as a philosopher writing about these questions, avoid having a view or at least saying explicitly that he was baffled? Even if it were true that all that matters, in concern about survival and so forth, is properly taken care of in the considerations Parfit has in mind, the problem what exactly is self-identity or what do we mean by 'personal identity' remains. Its importance may be diminished in some respects, but it cannot be wished away by just refusing to attend to it and diverting attention to other matters. Even if its ramifications are not as wide as has normally been thought, and as I shall be maintaining that they are, it remains an inherently important philosophical problem and, as most would admit, irrespective of questions of survival and accountability, a central one. Was Kant right or wrong, was Hume? I do not see how we can avoid tackling such questions or just decide to shut our eyes to their importance at least in philosophy.

The furthest that Parift is prepared to go in this article, on the question of what the distinct 'one-one relation' of identity involves, in the case of personal identity, is to cast doubt on the assumption that, in all cases, 'the question about identity must have an answer', that 'whatever happens between now and any future time, either I shall still exist, or I shall not'.[3] He is not certain how to disprove this belief, but he thinks he can make it seem implausible. His inclination is clearly to assimilate questions of personal identity to other identity questions — 'Is it the same machine?', 'Is it the same nation?' — here there is an arbitrary element and problematic cases at the edges. To this extent he is certainly giving an account of personal identity and taking sides on the question whether there is some finality in the view that I shall either exist or not exist at some future time. But on the whole he seems to leave the question open, or pass it by, according it at least enough distinctness as to declare it unimportant. What he is concerned to maintain is that, whatever is to be made of the question of identity, that has nothing to do with the important questions we ask about 'survival, memory, and responsibility'.[4] How, then, does he make that out? Let us turn to this question.

Parfit begins with a refinement upon the problem case envisaged by Professor Sydney Shoemaker, namely that of a transplant of one person's brain to the body of another, or a switching of brains. Most people would argue, Parfit holds, correctly in my view, that each person in this case would be the person whose memories and character he has in virtue of the way a brain makes this possible. But Professor David Wiggins had put forward a further variation, based upon the relative independence of the two halves of one's brain, the supposition, namely, that the two halves of one person's brain are separated and each housed in a different body. This can at least be imagined. But shall we then say that this is a genuine case of fission, that one person has now become two? Could it also be thought possible that one of the new persons is the same as the original? But how could it be one and not the other, especially if, as is supposed in this example, the two halves of the brain are exactly similar? Could the one original person be also both the new ones?

This latter supposition, it is urged, is not as absurd as might at first appear. For might we not have 'two bodies and a divided mind?' 'We can imagine a man having two simultaneous experiences, in having each of which he is unaware of having the other'.[5] We have in fact actual cases of this, as when the bridge between the two hemispheres of the brain is cut in the treatment of epilepsy. There are here 'two separate spheres of consciousness' but 'what is experienced in each is, presumably, experienced by the patient'.[6]

Parfit himself takes this further by supposing that 'the bridge between my hemispheres is brought under my voluntary control',[7] so that I can divide my mind at will. This would have its uses for example by my setting my two spheres of consciousness to work simultaneously on a problem to be solved in a hurry and later uniting my mind and selecting the best of the solutions proffered as remembered in my unified state of mind.

Parfit thinks that this possibility is a perfectly proper one to entertain, however improbable we may think it all in practice, and this has a considerable bearing on the further presentation of his views and the variations upon similar themes in the further discussions which this set off. But at this point, it seems to me, we get on to very questionable ground. It seems plausible enough in one way to suppose that two 'parts' of my mind could go on functioning at the same time without the one obtruding upon the other. Is not this happening all the time? Could I not be so lost in thought that, with that side of my consciousness, I am not at all aware of driving my car — the latter operation continuing quite well on its own? This is how we are often apt to think and to speak. If I am right, however, in what has already been maintained, this way of thinking is too simplistic. It is the one person who is deep in thought about some problem and who is driving the car. I do not drop my consciousness of the one in my concentration on the other. The mind just cannot be strictly divided in that way. If it happened, as was noted earlier, there would be a crash. What happens is that one matter occupies more the centre of my attention and demands more energetic pursuance. I do not become an automatic driver, it is myself who is driving the car and thinking out the problems, but the mental activity involved in the former is more subdued. There are, in short, no strictly separated spheres of consciousness. There is only the one consciousness diversified into various procedures undergone or enacted by the one person I am. There are no bits of my experience which can float away altogether from me. So, if it were possible for me to think out two solutions of the same problem at the same time, as I can listen to (or vaguely hear) the droning of a plane and compose this sentence, I could not be completely oblivious in the one case that the other was happening also.

We do not, therefore, in Parfit's example, begin to approach a situation of a strictly divided mind. Whatever we think of the possibilities of his example in itself, it does not set us on a path where there are really two persons and not one or a genuine fission. The one subject must be, however dimly in one respect, the subject of awareness in both cases.

Parfit himself does not, in fact, want to say that, in the example indicated, one person becomes, for some period, properly two, but only that this prepares the way for envisaging a situation when that would be the proper thing to say; and it is this which is helped by supposing it possible to imagine the same man 'having two simultaneous experiences, in having each of which he is unaware of having the other'.[8] My submission is that, in the strict sense, this is an impossible contingency, however much, for rough and ready purposes, we may speak in that way.

On the basis of the supposition just noted Parfit concludes that it is not obviously absurd to suppose that there could be two bodies and a divided mind, and, to this extent, we might conclude that this was the proper account to give of the situation where different halves of the brain had been housed in different bodies. I would also admit that we could say something of this sort, but only on the further vital qualification that it was the one mind which was continuing to function in these very different ways, and that it could not fail to be aware of what went on in both the new contingencies.[9]

Before we go further with that, let us see how Parfit himself proceeds. He maintains that, while it would not be absurd to envisage two bodies and a divided mind in the sort of limited situation he envisages, namely where the division is not protracted and ends in the reuniting of the two 'streams' of the mind, yet it would be absurd to entertain this notion if the mind were permanently divided and the halves developed, in their respective bodies, in different ways — 'they could live at opposite ends of the earth', they might meet and 'fail to recognise each other'.[10]

Here again the issue turns on whether one half of the divided mind could be totally unaware of what happens in the other. On my view this is not possible, though I think it is at least conceivable that one mind could be involved with two bodies at the same time. This is not a likely contingency — indeed our first reaction is to rule it out altogether. There are so many adaptations and difficulties to be overcome before it becomes remotely intelligible to us how this contingency might come about, due especially to the peculiarly close involvement with one particular body which is not only, in point of fact the case, but also a requirement of almost everything we do and undergo in an embodied condition. But there might be ways in which these difficulties could be surmounted, and I have already discussed them and the complications to be considered, in pages 106 and 113 of *The Self and Immortality*. The main point at the moment is that, as I also stressed in the context just noted, there would have to be awareness in the one 'life' of what goes on in the other, although much would be dim and little heeded, as already happens for many simultaneous experiences.

To put this again briefly, as it is very central to most that I would want to maintain against Parfit, it is, on the view I have already presented, impossible, in the nature of what it is to have experience, to have an experience without being aware, however unreflectively, of having it. If, therefore, in addition to all that goes on normally in my life, there is another embodied existence I have, perhaps far away as envisaged in Parfit's embroidering of Wiggins's example, then I just cannot, inherently cannot, be unaware of this. It is only, therefore, in a very restricted sense that one could 'have two bodies and a divided *mind*'. The mind could not be strictly divided, but only have two very distinct spheres and modes of operation.

For Parfit, envisaging as he does, a strictly divided mind, the question of identity becomes very acute in his case of a divided mind. We would have two persons, and we could not say they were identical without changing the concept of a person. In the context envisaged 'all the possible answers to the question about identity are highly implausible'.[11] The course to be followed therefore, it is maintained, is to give up the assumption that there must be a true answer to any question about personal identity, and, having thus taken away much of the significance of the question of identity, perhaps dispensed with it altogether, though this is not made explicit, then we prise the really important questions apart from any question of identity, leaving the latter 'with no further interest'.[12]

We come thus to the conclusion that 'the relation of the original person to each of the resulting people contains all that interests us — all that matters — in any ordinary case of survival'.[13] In terms of such relations it is not difficult to find a sense in which 'one person can survive as two'. We set aside, therefore, the idea of identity as 'all or nothing' and turn to relations, most of which are 'matters of degree'. 'The belief that identity *is* what matters is hard to overcome', but once the breach has been made, 'the rest should be easier to remove'.[14]

All that matters in judgements of identity is thus found to be psychological continuity, a principle that could operate even if there should be no bodily continuity. This is in sharp contrast with the move made by Bernard Williams in his discussion of someone seeming to be Guy Fawkes alive again, having the appropriate 'memories' etc. Williams insists that sameness of the body is necessary for identity. For Parfit we can pass beyond this and regard the new Guy Fawkes as the old one having survived or alive again provided the appropriate psychological continuity is assured. But what is it that is appropriate here? If there is not a 'one-one' relation of identity, what is to prevent the psychological continuity from being 'incomplete and arbitrary'?[15]

To deal with this we have to invoke the idea of 'psychological connectedness'. This consists in turn of 'direct psychological relations'. The most important of these concerns memory. It is normally taken as a logical truth that we can only remember our own experiences, but this does not debar us from framing a new concept 'q-memory'. This is found when we have an experience in all respects like memory except that it refers to an experience which someone else has had, my belief about this experience depending upon it in the same way as my 'memory of an experience is dependent upon it'.[16]

This is very attractive, but it begs the most important question of all. Suppose we did have some awareness of another person's experience as direct and dependable as memory of my own experiences, that is, not established by independent evidence and observation. We would presumably regard this as paranormal, but whether that is the appropriate term or not, we would still not have knowledge of the other person's experience *in the same way* as a memory is dependent on the experience remembered. For, whatever else we say about memory, in the strict sense, it seems to be quite essential to it that my assurance about what happened involves its having happened to *me*, I am able to recall it in the special way of memory just because I have lived through it myself. The alleged '*q*-memory' is therefore not a variant of memories at all, it could only be some peculiar way in which I become assured of what someone else's experience was like, somewhat like clairvoyance or telepathy; and these establish nothing about the relation of myself to other persons. I do not *have* the experience of another person in telepathy, that phenomenon provides no justification whatsoever for an alleged merging of persons. In memory, I recall the past experience as essentially an experience I have had, and however the dependability of it is finally understood, it would be quite off the mark to try to account for it regardless of what is most central, namely my having had the experience myself.

This is not a matter of words, of what we decide to call 'memory'. It is a case of what the phenomenon we do call 'memory' is like in itself. If we leave out what is vital, no other resemblances will help. This is what Parfit wholly repudiates. He does so quite expressly. 'When', he says 'I seem to remember an experience, I do indeed seem to remember *having* it. But it cannot be a part of what I seem to remember about this experience that I, the person who now seems to remember it, am the person who had this experience'.[17] I only make the latter assumption 'because I do not in fact have *q*-memories of other people's experiences.'[18]

Indeed, it is urged that all memories are initially '*q*-memories'. It only happens that I have them as memories of my own experiences. If I did begin to have 'q-memories' of other people's experiences, I would then be assured that someone had the remembered experience and 'have to work out who it was'.[19] 'Memories are, simply, q-memories of one's own experiences'.[20] In Wiggins's case of the two halves of a brain being housed in new bodies, we could ask of one of 'the resulting people' whether he had 'heard this music before' and he might reply 'I am not sure whether it was I who heard it, or the original person'.[21] Indeed, if only we started having q-memories of other persons' experiences, we could drop the concept of memory altogether.[22]

For this purpose, however, we would have to assume that some memories at least could 'come to me simply as beliefs about my past'.[23] It is this that seems to me to be a wholly unwarranted assumption. It is not in accord at all with what we find memory to be, which is not just some peculiar assurance about my past but the recalling of what my past was like, in some respect, because it comes as something through which I have lived myself. If it were not this it would be something radically different.

Let us turn now to the second major example of the relations in which connectedness consists. This is 'q-intentions'. 'It may be a logical truth that we can intend to perform only our own actions'.[24] But why not, again, 'redescribe' intentions as q-intentions which could allow us to 'q-intend to perform another person's actions'.[25] This seems to me a very daring line. One wonders to what excesses this convenient policy of redescription could lead. In the present case, the supposition proposed falls down irretrievably from the very start in respect of one matter which philosophers seem peculiarly apt to overlook today, namely that we just cannot intend to act, in the strict and proper sense, independently of, or ahead of, actual performance. We do, for rough and ready purposes, speak of forming intentions to do something in the future. I may, for example, say that I have formed a firm intention, or made up my mind or decided, to have my next holiday in Scotland. I was earlier very undecided, being much attracted to the idea of going to Italy. But I have now decided, my choice is for Scotland, that is where I will go. We are in fact forming intentions ahead in this way all the time, all our planning involves it. I intend to give a certain lecture in the autumn, to visit Emory University next year, to call to see a friend tomorrow. We would achieve little without planning, or intending ahead in this way.

And yet what do such intentions involve? In my intending to have my holiday in Scotland, I have firmly put out of my thoughts all consideration of going elsewhere. I have stopped thinking about it; my mind is made up. I also take the necessary steps, book my hotel, cancel other engagements etc. I do all that is necessary to do ahead. I make it such that going to Scotland will be the obvious and natural thing to do when the time comes, but I do not actually set myself to go until I do go. Circumstances could prevent me, or I could change my mind. Hell, we have all been told, is paved with good intentions, and New Year resolutions have a notorious habit of not being fulfilled. My dear father intended to give up smoking many times, but never did. It seems inherently impossible to do anything ahead of doing it, and though we might think it malicious of someone to harbour thoughts of murdering his rival, or in fact intending, in the present sense, to do so, we would not take this to be as bad as actually doing it, unless it were just his being prevented. He might change his mind on further thought, or 'when it comes to it', and we would certainly modify our moral condemnation accordingly.

The example that Parfit offers is again the Wiggins case of one person becoming two. As the original person he may intend to perform a certain action as one of the 'resulting people'. But, if I am right, he cannot intend in this way even in his own case, and if there is any sense in speaking in that way seriously at all, it could only be in the form of making such dispositions, including the set of his own thoughts, as would strongly (irresistibly?) induce one of his future selves to do something. I do not think that the notion of vicarious intending is a possible one, and the only way in which it would begin to be plausible would be if, in the Wiggins case, we took these to be one person with two bodies, not properly two resulting people.

Undaunted, however, Parfit anticipates that the vicarious operations could be extended to the situations where we 'q-recognise', 'be a q-witness' of what one has never seen, 'have q-ambitions, make q-promises and be q-responsible for'.[26] Indeed, this could pave the way to thinking experiences 'in a wholly "impersonal" way'.[27] That seems to me the appalling consummation of it, and in a much more disastrous way, for moral accountability and religion, than in the normal idealist elimination of the ultimate distinctness of persons. One wonders how far Parfit and those of like mind are prepared to take this, and whether they take the full impact of the consequence.

Parfit moves to the closing stages of his argument by setting out patterns of psychological continuity in terms of greater or lesser degrees of strength and closeness, ranging from those where the relation is strongest, namely the psychological connectedness of the 'direct' q-relations, to where it is so remote as to be of no account. In a case of fusion, the one person who results can, for example, q-remember the lives of the original two, and it would make sense therefore to speak of two persons now surviving as one. Alternatively, we are asked to think of beings who are like ourselves except that they reproduce by a process of natural division. These would all have some psychological continuity, but there will also be psychological connectedness which can 'vary in degree within a single life',[28] and in terms of the strength and closeness of this, and of other relations which are closest to it, we can distinguish cases where, for the purposes that matter we could say, for example, 'it was I who did that' and those where we could not do so. This gives us, in essentials, all that seriously counts when we are concerned about such matters as survival and responsibility. It is the closeness or degree of relation that really matters.

These possibilities are deployed with great ingenuity. But, for me at least, they produce little conviction. Even if we grant the central and most direct q-relations, and I have already urged that this is very questionable, it is by no means obvious that I should feel the most concern and affinity with those with whom I stand in the closest relations on Parfit's account. Suppose someone does have some peculiar direct awareness of what my experiences, or some of them, were like, does it follow that I would be more interested in him than others — members of my own family and circle of friends? The relation could be just a freak one, and I might well resent it. Again, if someone could q-intended that I do something, would not the natural reaction be to hold *him* solely responsible? How can these be properly his intentions *and mine* respecting the same actions, short of being strictly the one person and not two?

Suppose, again, one were assured that something pleasant (or unpleasant) was to happen to someone directly related to me in the present senses and were excited or dismayed as the case may be, this is *not the same* interest as I would have in some properly future experience of my own. I may, if I love someone deeply and am nobly motivated prefer some disagreeable fate to happen to me rather than to him, but this does not begin to be tantamount to the concern we have about some bad experience we may be likely to suffer ourselves. The latter turns on its being strictly my experience, just as my accountability turns on an action being strictly my own.

The distinctness of persons is not eliminated in the sort of relationships Parfit envisages, we are only diverted to arbitrary substitutes for it, and it seems to me that none of these, however close and ingeniously conceived, begins to do duty, in matters of survival and morals, for the way each person is, uniquely and finally, the person he is. To these implications of personal identity, in the strict sense, I shall return in the sequel to this book. In the meantime let us look at some of the ramifications of Parfit's procedures in the work of other writers who took their start from them.

Professor David Lewis maintains very ingeniously that, for ordinary purposes, that is excluding the notorious problem cases, there is nothing seriously at issue between the common-sense insistence on personal identity, as the crucial concern, and the sort of connectedness described by Parfit. What matters, he insists, when it comes to the point, is 'identity between the I who exists now and the surviving I who will, I hope, still exist then'.[29] This is not Parfit's view, he relies on the mental continuity and connectedness. 'One question, two answers'. But on David Lewis's view it all comes to the same thing. 'We need not choose, the answers are compatible, and both are right'.[30] The discrepancy is only 'formal'. 'What matters is that one and the same continuant person should have stages both now and later. Identity among stages has nothing to do with it, since stages are momentary. Even if you survive, your present stage is not identical to any future stage. You know that your present stage will not survive the battle — that is not disconcerting — but will *you* survive'?[31]

The answer is that 'identity among continuant persons induces a relation among stages: the relation that holds between the several stages of a single continuant person'.[32] This is 'the I-relation' and it is this that we must compare with the R-relation, defined as 'some definite relation of mental continuity and connectedness among person-stages'.[33] 'You wonder whether the continuant person that includes your present stage is identical with any of the continuant persons that continue beyond the battle'.[34] It is a question, in fact, of 'whether any of the stages that will exist afterward is I-related to — belongs to the same person as — your present stage'.[35] But Lewis claims that '*any stage is I-related and R-related to exactly the same stages*'.[36] The '*I-relation is the R-relation*'. For 'if we left out any stages that were I-related to one another and to all the stages we included, then what we would have would not be a whole continuant person but only part of one. For short: a person is a maximal I-inter-related aggregate'.[37] 'I cannot tolerate any discrepancy in formal character between the I-relation and the R-relation, for I have claimed that these relations are one and the same ... although the I-relation is not identity'.[38]

This comes extremely close to what I have myself been maintaining in somewhat different terms. The experience, 'the stage' as it is put here, belongs to the continuant person who is not himself the stage — the 'present stage will not survive the battle',[39] and I do not see how anyone could expect that. The continuant will, and that is what matters. This is why David Lewis holds that 'the I-relation does inherit much of the formal character of identity. But ordinarily the R-relation also is well behaved'.[40] The difficulty arises in the problem cases. How does that come about?

It comes about, in the case of fission for example, because the same stage may belong to two or more continuant persons, and these, very strangely, may be persons to a 'diminished degree'.[41] There may even be such a case that there is no such thing 'as *the* person of whom S is a stage'.[42] The I-relation may not have the formal character of identity in the problem cases, it may not be so if there is not 'some one continuant person of whom both S_1 and S_2 are stages'.[43] It might be possible to deal with this by supposing that there could be a 'partial overlap'[44] of continuant persons. This would preserve the I-relation and its transitivity. Some stages would be shared. But this is not possible, for there could then be more continuants than those that have stages at one time. In the case of fission for instance there would be two persons all along. A common 'initial segment' is ruled out because 'on the day before the fission only *one* person entered the duplication centre'.[45] The way out is to count, not by a method that agrees with the result of counting stages, but by 'a weaker relation' of 'tensed identity'. This is not an identity among continuants, but 'an identity-at-a-time'. 'So counting by identity-yesterday, there was only one (person). Counting by identity-today, there were two'.[46] 'There is a way of counting on which there are two all along; but there is another way on which there are first one and then two. The latter has obvious practical advantages. It should be no surprise if it is the way we prefer'.[47]

The justification for this is that in the problem cases 'we cannot consistently say quite all the things we feel inclined to. We must strike the best compromise among our conflicting initial opinions'.[48] In the case of fusion we can vary this by counting 'at t by the relation of identity-at-all-times-up-to-t'.[49]

The final conclusion is: 'if the R-relation is the I-relation, and in particular if continuant persons are maximal R-interrelated aggregates of person-stages, then cases of fission and fusion must be treated as cases of stage-sharing between different, partially overlapping continuant persons'.[50]

This idea of 'stage-sharing' and of 'partially overlapping continuant persons' seems to me to do the greatest violence to all we find ourselves normally disposed to think about ourselves. I am not a creature who can have a pain, let us say, by proxy. I have it while I have it or not at all. I cannot have it by sharing my existence with someone whose experience at some time I did not have at all. No amount of ingenuity will identify me with a person whose stage of being yesterday was not my own. The kind of identity posited here is entirely artificial. I am the same person as I was yesterday because I had the experiences I had yesterday. This is not a matter of convention but of fact.

This is why it seems to me out of the question for me to become two or more persons or for two persons to become me. It is not a question of ingeniously finding a way of representing this. I may be obliterated and two or more persons take my place or use my brain or neurological system — or a part of it. But if it is to be me it has to be wholly me as an integrated irreducible being, however changed or confused or many-sided. If another, who has part of my brain, shares my memories, he has to be me. I do not see how it can be otherwise in the nature of things, and I fail to see how David Lewis has provided any advance, in the problem cases, on the insurmountable difficulties they provided for Parfit.

This relates to the celebrated example of Methuselah, alleged to have lived nine hundred and sixty-nine years. The mental connectedness, which matters most for Parfit, fades with the passage of years. We are asked to suppose that they fade out completely in a matter of around 137 years. By the time this has been repeated nothing of the relationship that matters remains, and so for all that matters Methuselah by this time will be another person. This may be approached at least by very sharp changes of personality, brain damage, amnesia, conversions, senility. But quite independently of this Methuselah will have been many persons by the time he dies, in no way confined to the specific periods from which we begin to count for 137 years. 'There are infinitely many different 137-year segments that include all of Methuselah's stages on his 300th birthday'.[51] We may get out of this however, according to David Lewis, by counting in terms of 'tensed identity'. This leaves us only one person, for 'all the continuum many nonidentical continuant persons are identical-at-the-time-in-question'.[52] It follows however that, while identity cannot be a matter of degree, the t-relation may be so; and in this way we may come into line with Parfit's position. In cases of fusion for instance there may be relatedness to a reduced degree, and in the case of longevity, while we have to hold on to identity in the strict sense, the t-relation can become less significant or weaker, and could for all that matters fade altogether. At a certain point it matters as little to Methuselah now what his lot will be centuries hence as if he were not strictly the identical person he is. 'In this way personal identity can be just as much a matter of degree as the mental continuity of connectedness that matters in survival'.[53]

In effect the two positions are so similar as to make no difference — or at most a merely formal one. They invite the same comment. If I am assured that I shall live as long as Methuselah and shall spend the last two years of it in agony, I am certainly not so upset as I would be if threatened with the start of the same torture next week or even ten years hence. But I still know that it will be me and am disturbed by this fact just as much in David Lewis's account of things as in those of Parfit. Remoteness makes a difference, but as the centuries creep on my trepidation will increase because it will be *me*, I, the unique being that I am who will be the one that is going to suffer (or have a marvellous time) a thousand years hence.

In his subsequent comment on David Lewis's view,[54] Parfit points out that it all depends on the way different people might share stages when the alleged t-relation between them holds. But this, he points out, is not possible after fission when there really are two persons, 'two bodies and a divided mind'.[55] That the two minds seem to remember the same things will not save the situation, they must really remember and be the same person. Otherwise it is not identity that matters but something more akin to Parfit's own connectedness etc. David Lewis's case gains its plausibility by subtly importing into his crucial arguments the assumption I have been defending, that I really am strictly identical in all stages whether I remember them or not if they are stages of me, and therefore that it is this strict identity that matters. I may be peculiarly interested in someone very like me, who seems to have my memories etc. but he will not be me on that token alone.

What happens on Parfit's view has degrees. Psychologically this may be so, we have a 'discount rate' in respect to our distant future. But this does nothing to alter the facts of the case. Myself, as Methuselah, dying under torture, will still, in the fullest sense be me, however little it may trouble me now.

Professor Georges Rey has a somewhat different attack on the problem, though maintaining like Parfit that 'what matters to us is not identity over time'[56] and a one-one relation. She even suggests that more extensive duplication might be a more exciting prospect and that we may look forward to surviving as several different persons. In this way she agrees with Parfit that identity is not what matters, but rather our 'serious concern' with survival and what *this* involves. Identity may only come in in a secondary way, and she even goes so far as to say, in a moral instance, that moral blame could not be escaped by a person contriving his own fission. This is an incidental point, or relatively so; but I would certainly maintain that proper moral estimation, not always identical with what is more expedient in treatment for social and like purposes, would be very seriously affected if fission strictly meant that we had now two distinct persons. I would be disposed to say that there could be no moral disapprobation, affecting these two persons, of what had been done by the person we had before fission. He just would not be the same person any more, and one or more persons cannot be morally blamed on my view for what someone else had done. There would be nobody remaining accountable for what we could blame morally — it ended with the fission.

The matter would of course be entirely different if, as I have also envisaged, the one original person continues, functioning with different bodies. He would certainly retain his responsibility undiminished. But this is not the situation which Rey envisages. She does not think that it is identity that matters here, any more than in the case of survival.

On the other hand she certainly thinks that something does matter — 'what conditions underwrite our usual personal concern'?[57] We cannot regard this as purely arbitrary, a matter eventually of decision or persuasion, as might be the case, she supposes, in determining what is to count as humiliating or honourable. Even these matters are not wholly capricious; and certainly 'not all decisions are arbitrary'.[58] 'There must be some fairly well defined or definable basis, rooted in some general view, upon which we may systematically apply or withhold our concern'.[59] It is such a basis we must find in place of identity.

There is therefore no reason not to 'take seriously the kind of concern each person normally exhibits about all and only the person with whom she is identical'.[60] But there must be 'a basis' for this and that is what must be seriously sought. This is closely related to 'the relation that obtains between a person and usually only her own present experiences'.[61] However we may be gladdened or pained by other people's impending pleasures or pains, only each one can be personally concerned about his or her impending experience — 'only that person about only hers'.[62] This may be due to the fact that each person feels or has some unique privileged access to his own experiences, 'his present conscious states',[63] and this, as must be evident, is what I would maintain myself. But Rey will have none of this. We may be in error about our own experiences, and we have thus in all cases to ask, she claims, how we each enjoy a personally privileged epistemological stance, what natural conditions an entity must satisfy to enjoy[64] this epistemological stance. This is quite at odds with my own view that we are aware of these experiences in just having them, whatever their causes. She also claims that if there were telepathy we should be having the same 'privileged stance' to the conscious states of other persons, or even, most mysteriously to experiences, a pain for instance, which that other person does not have. There could indeed be 'inculcated' pains, induced by extreme concern or sympathy or in the bizarre case of a person's own writhings giving him the pains his wife is taken to have in labour. But this is quite artificial and gets us nowhere near actually having or undergoing the pains of another person. On the view I am defending it is just inherently impossible to have another person's experience in this way or to enter into it as it is for the person himself.

But what account then does Professor Rey offer of what others of us would regard as knowing an experience in having it? To deal with this she takes her cue from the well-known position of H. P. Grice, who says that a person has a particular experience, notably perception, if it is caused in some specific appropriate manner. If this means that the experience, and my identity as the being that has it, can be accounted for, in all essential terms, in terms of the causal conditions fully considered, it seems to me, as will be plain from what has been said already, that it is totally unacceptable. The experience just is what it is or what I find it to be, and my having it is also just that ultimate fact. But let us leave this aside and see how Rey proceeds. She claims that 'perception and privileged belief . . . must be the products of particular *kinds* of processes'.[65] If there seems to be a break-down of this it must be explained, as in the case of possible telepathy or of a person's having, or seeming to have, his wife's labour pains, in terms of peculiar causal conditions.

It is the causal condition that is thus really ultimate.

Certain behaviour is pain behaviour because it is typically caused in a specific way by a person's experiences of pains, which are also, typically, the causes of her abilities to relate and compare them, as of her privileged beliefs. Typically, that is to say, the evidence converges. Indeed, I do not think it would be far wrong to conceive of the network formed by these typical and appropriate kinds of causal chains, or mechanisms, as largely *constitutive* of the experiential relation: without any of the chains — without the appropriate causes for the (dispositions toward) privileged reports, the abilities to compare, the behaviour typical of the particular states — it would seem extravagant to suppose that there was, nonetheless, some full conscious experience. At least one would expect 'the experience' would be diminished. It is phenomena such as these, and especially their interrelations, that are the material, insofar as there be any material, of conscious life. Given, then, that this experiential relation is the object of our present tense personal concern, it would seem that the basis for that concern, at least at any particular time, consists in the normal functioning of that causal network.[66]

The functioning of that network entails personal identity 'at the time' 'and across time'. There might be difficulties where this leads to extensive division, but the key to solving them would be the experiential network. That is what matters for survival. Personal qualities, character, beliefs, even memory, will not suffice. For all these change, and even memory may be just 'seeming memory'. There may indeed be many persons at the present time, some in remote parts of space, hallucinating or otherwise having our conscious experience. But we would not be seriously personally concerned about such psychological duplicates. I should myself question this if the memory is not just a 'seeming memory', for reasons made clear already. But on the Gricean model followed by Rey there is no proper remembrance unless it is brought about in the appropriate way. Indeed she goes so far as to declare that 'it would certainly be surprising if the appropriate kind of causal chain could not stretch between persons whom, for independent reasons we might want to distinguish'.[67] What matters is '*that* the experience has been produced in a very particular sort of way'.[68]

In support of this view reference is also made to a possible objection to the 'mnemonic and psychological criterion' of identity, namely that we may dread or eagerly anticipate what may happen to us in changes like 'dreams, drugs, love affairs, meditations, religious conversions'[69] and so on, notwithstanding that we 'know full well we invariably will forget who we are during the dream', etc. The point is, I take it, that if we do so forget, our concern cannot turn on a psychological criterion. We must therefore look elsewhere to the way experiences are produced.

I have maintained, however, that, even if we do forget, in the dream for example, what our previous situation was like, or at least find our circumstances vastly changed, we do not in the least lose the basic sense of who we are, and the reason why I specially dread my having a nightmare or its like is that, whatever its precise course, it will be very unpleasant *for me*. In addition I do not think that, even in very wild dreams, we cut adrift altogether from awareness of the normal course of our lives. But on Rey's view, any psychological criterion comes down eventually to a 'causal chain', and this leads to our bodies. Causation requires some substance to sustain it. 'Dispositions require some underlying, continuous matter to be so disposed. Persons, their capacities, need embodiment'.[70]

This seems to me to be an unwarranted assumption, and I do not see why, along the lines of my chapter on 'The World of Thoughts Alone' in my *The Self and Immortality*, we might not have beliefs, characters etc., not sustained by any particular stuff at all. But for Rey this is inconceivable. 'Failure in the functioning of the mechanisms of our personal embodiment is failure of ourselves to be embodied: we die, even if the matter of which we are composed endures'.[71]

The most important ingredient in the required network are normally 'our brains and nervous systems' — not just flesh and bones, and Sperry's work is thus much more disturbing philosophically than that of Christiaan Barnard. But we are not quite dependent even on the crucial stuff of our bodies, not even the continued identity of the brain, for the latter, as in Sperry's examples, can be dissipated, but the causal network must survive. 'The basis of what matters to us, in our personal survival, seems to consist in the *not necessarily identical continuity of our functioning personal embodiment*'.[72] The underlying stuff could even be other than material substance, though this seems not to be taken very seriously in the slighting tone of the reference to 'rare ectoplasms distilled in the laboratories at Duke or in the jungles of Brazil'. The point is 'not that we must be made of the stuff science has so far found; but that we must be made of *something*'.[73] On this view reincarnation is not to be strictly ruled out, and Catholics are thought to have an advantage over Protestants, presumably because they are supposed to attach more importance to the resurrection of the body.

What matters is, in any case, the continuity of the causal network, whatever the stuff that sustains it. But *why* should this concern us so much? Does it not matter much more that I should be myself whether sustained by some personal network or not? We know very little about the network, it is a matter for specialists, but we all have ideas of certain kinds of experience and their being enjoyed by us. This is what strictly concerns us, and it is quite peripheral for normal concern and expectations how these come about. Would it give me any cause for anxiety or enjoyable anticipation apart from the expected experience, to know that the network would persist? If the same experiences were to be produced in some other way, as might well be in another mode of existence, would this be cause for any serious concern? Professor Rey concludes with the suggestion that with the evanescence 'in our concerns and accompanying differences in the distinctions we find useful to draw', we may some day find it quite natural to be 'indifferent to one's own, as opposed to anyone else's, personal fate'.[74] The reverse seems to me to be the case.

An interesting and ingenious variation on these themes is provided by Professor John Perry. He inclines to the view, though not wholly committed to it, that personal existence depends on physical continuity, but he also maintains that what matters in our concern about survival and our own future states is different. Bodily identity, though not 'a necessary nor a sufficient condition for a personal identity', is 'nevertheless importantly involved in our concept of personal identity . . . The stable relation between persons and bodies is, in this sense, not an accident although purely contingent; if the P-relation', which *explains* the relations (H-relations) which are 'stages of a single human being', 'was not generally accompanied by, and causally related to, the H-relation, we would not have the concept of a person we do have'.[75] '*Having the same brain* is at least a promising candidate for the P-relation'.[76] But this does not explain the special concern we have about what happens to us in the future. If, by pushing a button I can prevent someone being in great pain tomorrow, I shall normally be very keen to do so. 'But intuitively, if the person is *me* I will have more reason, or perhaps special reasons, for pushing it'.[77] What can be the reason for this?

The reason, we are told, is in terms of my projects for tomorrow. If I am in great pain I shall not be able to accomplish the projects I have in mind for tomorrow. 'If I am not in pain tomorrow, I will contribute to the "success" of many of my projects: I will work on this article, help feed my children, and so forth. If I am in great pain, I will not do some of these things'.[78] I should myself have thought there was a great deal more than this to it. It is not just my projects that will suffer, I shall myself have to endure great *pain*. But let us keep to the importance of the continuity of our projects. This is something which, at least at one level, we have in mind in thinking of the continuity of a person. Our interests do sometimes undergo dramatic changes, but generally we retain the idea of a person having 'much the same desires, goals, loves, hates'[79] most of the time. It was stressed earlier that this is one important sense of being the same person. Moreover, no one is as likely as I am to have the same concern for these projects, 'love my children, vote for my candidates, pay my bills, and honour my promises, as me'.[80]

But this does not wholly cover the case. It is not impossible for someone else to do all the work in question just as well. Indeed, someone else may even do it better. I would still be more struck with horror at the knowledge that I, rather than the sustainer of my projects, will be hit by a truck tomorrow — because I would think of the dreadful 'event as happening to me'.[81] Why should this be?

The answer is given in terms of 'identification'. 'A person *identifies* with the participant in a past, future, or imaginary event, when he imagines perceiving the event from the perspective of the participant; that is, when he imagines seeing, hearing, smelling, tasting, feeling, thinking, remembering, and so on, what the person to whom the event happened did (or will or might) see, hear, smell, taste, feel, think, remember, and the like, as the event occurs'.[82] I can imagine Napoleon losing the battle of Waterloo, but not with any of the sorts of details mentioned.

Indeed, we may not identify in the sense in question with many things in our own past or futures. When we do 'the memory or expectation' has more 'impact' upon us. I keep my equilibrium while I just know of the pain that is going to happen to me tomorrow and am not terrified till I start to imagine it. When I do so, this does not give me more reason for pushing the button that will spare me more pain, but it makes it more likely that I will do so. Identity is not a condition of identification. Nor do I have to imagine myself the same as the participant with whom I identify. There are in fact no limits to our ability to identify with various participants. But we are much more likely to identify with ourselves than others and with our own 'future selves'. One of the reasons for this is that the participant with whom we identify may be significantly different from us (members of another species, perhaps, in some remote part of space) and, secondly, that we ourselves are in a better position to watch out for ourselves than others. Some may want a more metaphysical reason for wanting to get to the bottom of our concern for our future self. But for Professor Perry the empirical account he has offered provides an adequate 'evolutionary derivation of the facts explained' and generally meets the demand for explanation of why we have 'a preponderance of reasons for actng in our own behalf, and strong motivation for acting on them'.[83]

There still seems for Perry something incomplete about this. The reasons he has mentioned might be equally good for sparing someone else the pain. But there must be 'special' reasons in my own case. The main reason is in terms of projects that I have which no one is likely to complete as I wish them done. This would be strongest if it included 'my being in a certain state' (a 'private project'), for that clearly requires that I be alive myself and not a substitute. We have many such 'private projects' and also some 'ego projects' which simply require my existence. In these ways it becomes important 'not merely that this article be completed, but that it be completed by me'. Why should this matter on Perry's theory? It matters partly because I am not certain that it will not be 'ill-completed and partly because it may be connected with many of my other non-private projects'. But suppose these doubts are set at rest. Suppose that everything I will do, 'for the rest of my life, will be done and done as well, and done in just the same way, by someone else. Still I want that I complete it and not this benign impostor'.[84]

The answer is in terms of 'habit'. 'Usually surviving is the only way to achieve a good part of what we want done',[85] and we thus naturally want to survive. Also we identify better with our own doings than with those of others. This 'habit' too is 'ingrained in us by the demands of evolution and its utility for achieving our purposes in ordinary circumstances',[86] and it explains, in part at least, the more metaphysical concern we are still inclined to have. Perry denies outright that more than this is involved in 'my desire that it be I who finish the article' 'not only in the normal circumstances but even in the metaphysical'.[87] He affirms that the only justification for my concern for a private project is 'a derivative one' — I do not really expect others to succeed as well. The real explanation is 'the result of habit as it is, and the demands of evolution'.[88]

If we remain reluctant to accept this, the explanation is that it is peculiarly hard to believe that my projects will be carried out as I want them by another, or to find adequate justification for this. A supporting reason is that so much that I wish to accomplish and complete depends on things in my past history, including things that only I can remember. My duplicate will be lying or deceiving himself if he declares or implies that he remembers things which I did. The only way of avoiding this is of his having 'been produced' from me which is only meaningful through 'a reliable causal relation'.[89] If a team of scientists invent some way of disposing of me (because I have an incurable disease perhaps) and creating in secret a duplicate that 'will simply take over my life', then 'he would not be me'.[90] 'But on my (Perry's) account, I would have the very same legitimate reasons to act now so as to secure for him future benefits as I would if he were me'.[91] This is not a defect to be charged to Perry's account 'but an insight to be gained from it'.[92]

If, after amnesia, I were to change and become a very disagreeable or reprehensible person, I would still care about this person and at moments perhaps be ashamed of him (certainly if I were told beforehand what would happen) but this, it seems, is to be explained entirely in terms of habit. The supposed '"ineffableness" of the fellow who would survive' 'when it is not the remnant of a bad theory of personal identity, is simply the shadow of the enormous contribution that we are in the habit of expecting ourselves to make to the projects we have'.[93]

The importance that we do actually ascribe to identity is thus derivative. I will have many relations with people with whom I will identify (in Perry's special sense). 'But it is incredibly unlikely that I should have all of them (the relationships to others) I will have to myself, to anyone else'.[94] If, however, the 'many relations', or more strictly all of them, are guaranteed, if Smith (in the brain rejuvenation case) 'can expect to have as tight a web of special relationships to the survivor of the operation as personal identity in its purest form could provide', this 'is all that need matter to him'.[95]

Now there can be little doubt that Professor Perry's view is sound in important respects. Our projects do matter to us, and in some cases (the statesman, the reformer, the artist, the man of letters, the scholar, for example) these projects are of immense importance and such that, in many cases the instigator of them would sacrifice his own life to ensure their fulfilment. If an author is told that he will be dead within a few days, one of the matters that will grieve him most will be that the novel he is halfway through, and which is going well, will never be completed, and certainly not completed as he would have it. But this, I submit is not of the same order as my concern about my total extinction. In some cases of acute suffering extinction may be the preferable course. But short of some calamity of this kind being in prospect, most of us would wish to survive as ourselves however ruined some of our major projects may be. In a long prison sentence, or sustained illness, I may accomplish little of what I had previously been expecting to achieve. But I shall be having some experiences, and not all of them unpleasant or frustrating to the point of being unendurable. Most convicts would prefer a long or life sentence to execution. We are concerned that we should be having some experiences and that they should be had by us — by me, this same individual that I am now.

It would be comforting to know that someone would complete my novel and do it superbly well, that, if other people survive in a future existence, they will enjoy loving and co-operative relations with the friends of whom death has now deprived me. I am concerned that my parents will be happy, and that their sanctified postmortem experience will continue to expand and be enriched. But this is not of the same order at all as that *I* shall meet them, that I shall enjoy again their manifestations of their love for me. This is the sort of expectation which religious people have normally had, and I think they are right and certainly interpreting the New Testament aright. Projects, short-term or long-term, may have the greatest importance. Life would be dreary to the extent of pointlessness without them. But projects are one thing, my own continuation as the distinct person I am (and also in distinctive relations to other persons) is quite another. In hoping to survive in some form, after my demise in this world, I am hoping that it will be me, not some copy or duplicate, but the same consciousness, the same strict identity as I have now, even if I have only dim memories of what I am now or pass beyond the importance they may have for me now — a contingency which I however think wholly unlikely in the matters that are of greatest moment in my present existence.

7 Some Reluctant Concessions

The first part of this chapter will be concerned with two statements of a position which comes very close to the view advanced in this book, and seems to make substantial concessions to it. But they are also statements which shy away from full acceptance of the view I have presented and call for some supplementation in the form of some more explicit account of personal identity than the recognition of it in its uniqueness and finality by each individual in his own case. The statements in question appear in two related articles, the second of which takes its cue from the first and seeks to build further upon it. These are (1) an article by Professor J. A. Brook in the *American Philosophical Quarterly* for July 1975 entitled 'Imagination, Possibility and Personal Identity' and (2) 'Who I am' by Professor Don Locke in the *Philosophical Quarterly* for October 1979.

Two statements in the first part of Professor Brook's article give us the clue to his general concern. He declares, with a bow to Leibniz, that:

> One key part of general identity theory would, if correct, be enough to show that any concept of identity, at any rate, has necessary conditions, one of which is that wherever identity is, there also something non-trivially sufficient for it must occur.[1] Again: I hope to show that the presence or possibility of personal identity *does* require the presence of something different from identity, namely some minimal connection between the persons being identified.[2]

With these aims in mind Brook turns to the question of 'what a person can imagine concerning himself'[3] and the claim that 'I can refer to my present self as myself without supposing, in the act of referring, that I have any properties (except, perhaps, the proper

125

ty of being a subject of experience)'.[4] Such references are 'non-ascriptive'. 'In the same way, apparently, I can non-ascriptively refer to past persons (in memories or supposed or imagined memories) as myself, and to possible future persons (in day-dreams etc.) as myself. That is, I need not suppose in my reference that the remembered (or apparently remembered) person or the imagined past or future person has any properties whatsoever (except, trivially, the property of being me and, perhaps, of being a subject of experience'.[5]

It is admitted that it is tempting to admit that one can refer in 'the imagination to an imagined past or future person as oneself while supposing no connection with one's present self different from identity'.[6] I can in this way 'imaginatively identify the person they called Napoleon with myself'.[7] But, it is maintained, this does not entail that I do not *suppose* any connections. In using terms such as 'I', 'me', 'myself' to refer to one's present self, we may not be making explicit reference to one's own properties or even believe that one has them. But one must know how to use such terms and must thus have a grasp of the conditions for using them, for example the condition of referring to a subject of experience. To use such terms 'intelligibly' one must suppose such conditions satisfied without strictly knowing or thinking about them.

When, moreover, we claim identity with some person other than one's present self, we must, it would seem, 'make suppositions non-trivially relevant to that imagined identity, i.e. suppositions of connections different from identity'.[8] To this the reply might be made that the only relevant condition is that the person is me. But this is said to be unintelligible. For, in that case 'there would be no difference between that person being you and his not being you'.[9] To this, in turn, the reply might be made that 'there would be a difference; but nothing further can be said about it'.[10] This is the submission which Brook sets out especially to challenge, claiming that 'imagining identity entails supposing in the imagination connections different from identity'.[11] This may not be prominent in imagining oneself identical with some past or future person — indeed it may be overlooked; but 'that is not enough to show that one *has* supposed no such connection, nor therefore that it is logically possible that one will be a future person with whom one is not otherwise connected'.[12]

To reinforce this Brook turns to the case of 'thought-

experiments in which one has maximal reason to believe that one
is supposing no connection (other than identity) between oneself
and a future person whom one is to imagine as oneself'.[13] I am
thus required to imagine myself the future King of China. It is
not enough, for the purpose in question, to imagine myself
becoming a future King of China. We have to imagine that 'the
person you are' and the future King are one person. This might
seem easy — 'I have just done so', one might reply, 'I have
imagined giving the orders and feeling the pride etc.' But what
one really does, it is further urged, is to imagine oneself, or 'what
one can only *call oneself*'[14] witnessing and having and doing.
That does not amount to 'the person referred to in the imagination' being 'the person doing the imagining'.[15] It may be no
more than oneself imagining '*from the standpoint* of being the
person witnessing or having or doing so-and-so'.[16] But this is not
the same as imagining that person to be oneself.

Indeed, in one way it is perfectly easy to imagine oneself being
another person. I could imagine being a doctor and doing the sort
of things a doctor (or a lawyer) does. I could imagine being
Napoleon, that is I might dress like him and speak as I suppose he
spoke, I might even do this on the field of Waterloo; this is the
sort of thing a clever actor does. Some can do it more effectively
than others, but it presents no inherent difficulty. Childrens'
games involve it. But this does not amount to imagining that you
are the other person, even in the case of Henry Irving — we are
told — so entering into the part that he continued off-stage
walking about with uplifted sword. There certainly is a difference
between imagining (or should we say 'pretending') in this
ordinary sense and seriously imagining oneself as Napoleon or a
character in fiction. For here, in the ordinary sense, there is no
deep suspension of belief.

One can therefore concede a difference between imagining, in
the common or garden sense, that one is Napoleon, even doing
this very intensely and thoroughly, and so imagining oneself as
Napoleon that one seriously takes oneself to be Napoleon. But is
the latter impossible? Are there not crazy people who do just that?
And moreover, whatever may be the truth here, however difficult
it may be in fact or practice for me to so sever my connection with
my present environment and all I remember about myself, as to
seriously take myself to be Napoleon or anyone else, that is very
different from my being able to *conceive* of my circumstances,

feelings, actions.etc., being so changed that they are not discernibly different from those of someone else, a fictitious or real character, famous or ordinary, and yet its being *me* to whom all this has happened. If I am the cobbler I can readily imagine that I have actually, and not in simulation or pretence, become the prince. It would still be me to whom this has happened, and normally I could be fully aware of the fact even though I could not convince anyone else.

This is what Brook seems to be really challenging. I agree with him that I can never imagine — or even properly understand — what it would be for me to *be* someone else. Indeed, this is what I especially stress. I just could not be other than myself, being myself is ultimate, as I find in the fact of being myself. But in all that appertains to me beyond this I could change, and there appears to be no inherent difficulty in imagining that this has come about. This is what Brook is reluctant to admit. I can imagine being X, that is conjure up the sorts of thing that is happening to X, but, as I have also stressed, this is not imagining my being X. Brook holds that for this to happen there must be '*some* imagined connection'.[17] This could be memories, or imagined bodily, causal or spatio-temporal continuity.

Now awareness, or some imagination at least, of such connection (memories are what I would stress) would be necessary for me to be aware, and accordingly to imagine being aware, that I had become Napoleon or a future King of China. But, on my view, I might have been or, in the second case become, either of these without retaining knowledge of my present condition. I might be reincarnated — and for this reason, I have argued elsewhere,[18] the idea of reincarnation, without any knowledge of our past existence, is at least perfectly conceivable, whatever the strength of the case for it — evidential or metaphysical — may be. I would simply have the same self-awareness in my new existence, or in some radically transformed state, that I have now.

For Brook, however, there has to be added some 'further connection' other than my unique self-awareness and the full present state of the person I imagine myself to be. There are two possibilities here. I can imagine being the other person — and we can all fairly easily do this, enter into his feelings etc. — but, secondly, to imagine being strictly identical with the other person, this is something else, and so far fine, but Brook claims that we cannot thus 'imagine identity with some imagined person while imaginatively supposing no connection different from identity to him'.[19]

It is the neglect of this, not only in the case of Chisholm, standing by the ultimacy of self-identity as such, but also of Bernard Williams unable to decide as to which of two possible persons in the future he should, from the point of self-interest, be most concerned to benefit, that causes the trouble. The connection need not be memories, indeed 'the connection you suppose need not be anything specific'.[20] I might have no notion what it was, except that it was relevant to identity. I might believe all current theories of identity to be false but have no notion what to replace them with.

This is a very weak conclusion, and it suggests to me that Professor Brook has been driven to a somewhat desperate and lame conclusion because of some ingrained reluctance to break with contemporary fashion and reject what he describes as the 'strict' theory of identity when the main force of his arguments points strongly towards it. There would have to be something more than the properties of the imagined person, but he will not rest content here with merely saying that one would just have to *be* the identical person having them; and thus, not being able to specify anything further, or be happy about any such specification, Brook falls back on the rather desperate move of claiming that there must be *some* connection. Thus he declares: 'A great many things necessary for identity may be missing from what is actually imagined. That an identity with a future person has been imagined without imagining (or supposing) those things proves nothing to the contrary'.[21] The suppositions may be unnoticed, and we may remain very uncertain what they are. And this in turn opens up the possibility, in the absence of strict identity, that the connection could be such that I no longer persist as strictly the same person. We do not have to hold on to the 'notion of a designator ("I") whose designation could unambiguously persist as the same person if it persists at all'.[22] 'My ability to achieve reference to myself as myself without ascribing any identifying property to myself does not tell me of a thing, namely myself, which must be projected into the future always me, always unambiguously identical with the person I now call me, until its unambiguous death'.[23] A future person need not be strictly me or not me. He may end 'by elanguescence! Or by becoming another person. Or for that matter by becoming two'.[24]

And so, once the interest has been shifted to 'some connection', we are indeed back again with the possibilities we queried in the last chapter of the fusion or the merging of persons which I have argued to be inherently impossible from the way we know ourselves, each in his own case, to be the persons we are.

It is at this point that Professor Don Locke takes up the problem from Professor Brook. He sets out in full agreement with Brook that there is all the difference in the world 'between imagining being Napoleon and imagining that you are Napoleon'.[25] The first of these is straightforward, as we have already seen. I can imagine what it 'would be like to have seen what Napoleon saw, to have done what he did, thought what he thought, felt what he felt'.[26] There are difficulties in trying to reconstruct in this way what someone's life is like 'from the inside' but they are psychological or epistemological and do not threaten 'the very coherence of the enterprise'.[27] That only happens when I try seriously to imagine that I am Napoleon instead, in this case, of Don Locke.

The proper account of this, it seems to me again, is that it is inherently impossible for one person to be or to become another, and that to try to imagine it is to try to imagine the impossible. As the author himself puts it, 'whatever I succeed in imagining whoever I succeed in imagining myself to be, that person will always be myself, even if I am Napoleon; I cannot imagine that I am anyone or anything, without imagining that it is me'.[28] What I can do is simply imagine 'not that this present individual is Napoleon, but that in using "I" I refer not to this present individual but to Napoleon instead'.[29]

According to Brook, the only way that the present individual could be also Napoleon, would be if some connection, 'the missing ingredient', could be established between the present individual and Napoleon, for example that Napoleon had escaped and lived long enough to figure now as Don Locke. But this is inadequate, for it would simply mean that it was strictly the same individual in both cases.

At the same time Don Locke wants to give some account of why I could not in any other sense be another person, and he offers us something other than the finality of self-identity as we seem normally to recognise it. How does he proceed?

He proceeds by turning instead to the question of when an alleged autobiography would no longer be a proper autobio-

graphy of oneself or a serious candidate for it. Now a proper autobiography of Don Locke would tell us correctly what his life had
been like, where he was born and brought up, educated, what
jobs he had held and so on. But it is also conceivable that his life
could have run a different course. Instead of becoming a philosopher and academic teacher, he might have become a librarian.
Indeed his life might have run a more radically different course.
He might have been abducted or adopted at birth and taken to
some quite different environment from that in which he was
actually nurtured and be engaged in some work very far removed
from that which occupies him now. That would give us a very
different autobiography, but it is still a possible autobiography of
Don Locke. Things might have happened that way. This gives us
a 'different possible' or 'alternative' biography. But there are also
biographies which would have to be biographies of someone else
— if of anyone. They could not be biographies of Don Locke.
These are labelled 'distinct biographies'.

The question then is when a biography, which was not a sound
or genuine one, would still be a possible or alternative biography,
and when it would have to be regarded as a 'distinct' biography,
that is could not be conceived as a biography of Don Locke, but,
if at all, of some other individual.

Now there are some things which I could rule out of a possible
biography of me as I have come to know myself now and as
obvious evidence suggests. No training, however early it started,
could have got me to be an Olympic winner of a gold medal. I
might be brought to run much faster than I ever did run, but it is
just not in me to run like an Olympic winner. I just do not have
those bodily aptitudes, any more than I could become a famous
singer. On the other hand, if I had been born with a different
endowment or different physique and capacities, I might have
become these things.

This suggests that the point from which to start is birth. 'Biographies qualify as alternatives so long as they share the same
beginning, whereas if they have different origins they will be
distinct'.[30] If I were abducted at birth, my entire life might have
been very different. All sorts of things are possible in this way,
and they are features of what my life could have been. Even so,
Professor Locke does not think identity of birth altogether
sufficient. I might have been born a week earlier or later. So we
are pushed back to conception, 'of which particular combination

of sperm and egg he is the product'. But even this is not strictly necessary. It is simply that we are strongly inclined to suppose that subsequent histories cannot be the same once the beginnings are different — the range of possibilities are bound to be different in some ways. But we might, by some very unusual chance, get off with the same genetic make-up even if born of different parents. So that what really matters is the genetic make-up.

Kripke, it is noticed, takes a different line on this, although he offers no strict argument for it, only an 'intuition', whatever that word, so familiar but so obscure in very recent philosophy — as it was not forty years ago — may mean. Locke has a different 'intuition' (hunch?). If we imagine that the Queen of England had in fact been the daughter of Harry Truman but passed off from the start as the daughter of George VI and then living the life of the Queen just as it has been lived, we would not, according to Locke, be imagining the life history of some other woman than the Queen. 'If the difference were solely a difference of parentage, if the rest of her history were very much as it has been, I can see no reason to deny that it is still that same person'.[31]

At this point the writer seems to waver. 'It is difficult to see how Harry Truman could father a daughter with Elizabeth's face' but 'if we start with the mature Elizabeth, sitting on the throne, it does seem possible to envisage a different past for her, in which this very woman is the child of different parents'.[32] This leads to a different account of what would be 'the mark of alternative biographies', namely that they should be for a time, indistinguishable'.[33] 'Instead of speaking of biographies as converging or diverging, let us speak of them as *coinciding* at those points where they are the same'.[34] Biographies may thus coincide for a period, they 'are alternatives only for the period during which they do coincide'.[35]

That, however, is not thought to be quite satisfactory. For 'biographies which diverge remain alternatives even after they no longer coincide'.[36] We are thus brought to the conclusion 'that differing biographies qualify as alternatives when and only when they have coincided, and afterwards, but not before'.[37] 'Biographies coincide at those moments or periods when their subjects are indistinguishable from each other'.[38] This is weakened however to the extent that only 'sufficient important things' be true of both cases for them to be regarded as alternative biographies, and they must coincide for 'a significant period of time'.[39] It is also claimed that the alternative biographies must coincide at some sufficiently early point, however much they may differ thereafter.[40] This, as the author himself puts it is 'intolerably vague'. If my closing year in a geriatric ward coincides closely with that of an Australian journalist, a man 'differing in almost every (other) respect'[41] from me, there is no temptation to think that our cases might present 'possible (alternative) biographies of one and the same individual'. 'The coincidence' must occur sufficiently early for the biographies to qualify as alternatives through the greater part of the individual's existence.

The main significance of this discussion, for the question of personal identity and related questions, appears to be that, if my life had in fact taken any of the courses regarded as alternative biographies, I would still have to be regarded as the same person. Identity is here made to depend on some continuity with one's origins. It is not clear to me whether it is seriously envisaged that the coincidences described would involve a genuine merging of persons. That would seem to be difficult to reconcile with the insistence on a common genetic origin, and one would also expect it to involve, as the case is envisaged in this article, a very complete coincidence of physical as well as psychological states and properties, such as is extremely unlikely to happen. The upshot seems to be that, when we have followed all the distinctions and qualifications, the decisive factor is some psychological and physical continuity of the sort envisaged already in the papers we have considered earlier, and this seems well brought out in a concluding note.

In this note the issue is firmly returned to the question of spatio-temporal continuity, the crucial issue being what degree of resemblance is required to ensure this. Much importance seems to be attached to the suddenness with which drastic changes may occur. We are told:

If my eyes were suddenly to change colour, if I were suddenly to age biologically by three weeks, I do not think we would regard those discontinuities as conflicting with the claim that one individual had endured through the change ... But if the differences are such that, were some actual individual to change instantaneously in those respects, we would no longer be prepared to regard him as the one continuing individual, then those differing biographies cannot be regarded as coinciding, even in the weakened sense.[42]

In coming to this conclusion Professor Locke takes no account of phenomena like dreams where far-reaching and sometimes fantastic changes occur. As I have maintained earlier, however strange the dream we do not in the least lose the sense of our own particular consciousness or individuality — all this is happening to me. There is also the case of reincarnation. This, I have argued, is perfectly conceivable, even without presupposing that one has any memory of a previous existence. It would involve all the changes Don Locke has in mind, but it would not preclude identity in the sense of the same consciousness of the being that I am.

In his own reference to reincarnation early in his paper[43] Don Locke finds no difficulty in one's imagining oneself to be Napoleon in the sense of thinking myself into the mind and experiences of Napoleon, or that Napoleon had lived much longer than we thought and emerged on the public scene in a vastly altered form, but I could not imagine myself to be Napoleon in the sense of taking the person I actually am now to be Napoleon. I would simply be using 'I' in a peculiar way, for it is just not possible for the individual I know myself now to be to be also another individual. I can only be the one person I am. This is what I urged is promising in the cases of Brook and Locke. But instead of taking the full, and to me obvious, import of this, namely that the person one is is final or ultimate, whatever drastic changes we undergo in character or circumstances, both writers seek other ways of accounting for what is, I believe, an initially quite sound insight which they are determined to explain in various ingenious ways that do not question the understanding of identity in terms of some form of continuity or like feature of our existence.

My own submission here is that the failure of these attempts, and the strains to which they put their authors, should be strong inducements to reflect again and consider more seriously the claim that one's failure to seriously think oneself any other person than one is, notwithstanding being able to imagine oneself another person in the senses readily admitted, namely giving oneself his role and attitudes etc., is simply due to the finality of each one's consciousness of being the one person he is whatever fate or change of circumstance befall him, now or hereafter.

If I were in fact to find myself in some future state after my death, there would certainly be *some* drastic changes. I would no longer have my present body, presumably reduced to ashes in a crematorium.[44] I might have another body, resembling my present body, or function in some different medium not known to me now, or, as I have also considered in *The Self and Immortality* (Chapter 8, 'A World of Thoughts Alone'), no body at all. These would all be drastic changes, some more severe (and for that reason perhaps less probable) than others; but in each case there would have to be the consciousness of being the person I now find myself to be which I have now. Whether I linked this with memories of a previous existence is a further matter. Without that I could not think of myself as the person who had lived out this present life, and that is I think a strong reason for expecting that if a future existence were to be conferred upon us, it would involve some linkage with my present life.

These are matters for further discussion elsewhere. All that needs to be noted now is that the possibilities I have noted seem all to be ruled out by the positions adopted by both Brook and Don Locke. Notwithstanding the insistence that to imagine myself someone else would fall short of imagining being someone else, and the impossibility of being someone else, they understand this additional factor of just being the person I am in terms of some properties by which I am to be identified such as continuity or an initial common start to all the experience and doings which can properly be said to be mine. They come close to what seems to me the nub of the matter, and then shy away again in line with the more common way of treating the matter today.

I turn now to a somewhat different approach to the subject I have been discussing, an approach which also, in its own way, comes very close to the position I advocate, but which also, when it comes to the crunch, drifts away from it and, it seems to me, fails to do the fullest justice to the insights which make the concessions persuasive and significant. This is found in the paper contributed by Mr John Foster to the volume of essays published in honour of Professor Sir Alfred Ayer, *Perception and Identity*.

The first part of Mr Foster's essay is remarkably far removed from what one has come to expect from impressive Oxford philosophers in days still not very far distant from the publication of *The Concept of Mind* and its considerable impact. It appears after all that we have at least to come to terms in some way with Descartes again.

Mr Foster declares that 'the concept of a person'[45] 'is to be analysed in terms of the special way in which two logically separable components, a body and a mind, combine'.[46] 'The person himself, though qualifying for personhood only in virtue of this combining of body and mind, is essentially mental and only contingently corporeal'.[47] This is 'what we may call the *dualistic doctrine of the person*'.[48] 'The subject of consciousness is, as Descartes conceived him, a simple mental continuant, a pure ego, not requiring a body for his existence, but possessing that body with which his mind thus causally combines'.[49] In these terms there is rejected the notion that 'the concept of a person is logically primitive'[50] and the avoidance attempted in that way by Sir Peter Strawson of the traditional problems of body and mind.

'I do not see', Mr Foster adds, 'how to avoid, even in the case of action, the sharp contrast between mental and physical states'.[51] We know of our own mental states 'without observation or inference', and this 'self-ascription' is not, as Strawson had insisted, logically bound up with 'other-ascription'. The latter is not a 'precondition of self-ascription'. 'The most that self-ascription logically requires is the capacity to conceive of the existence of other subjects of the same type as oneself and with similar mental states'.[52] We recognise such mental states, in the case of other-ascription, not by analogy, but, as Mr Foster sensibly points out, on the basis of what would 'provide the most plausible explanation of' a body's 'behaviour'.[53] The intention is ascribed, when we see someone coiling a rope, 'as an interpretation of the movement. In other words, we discern in action a point where the co-ascription of mental and physical attributes has, or seems to have, a natural intelligibility'.[54]

So far so good. But Mr Foster does not stop here. He feels that he must find some means of giving a further account of personal identity which is nonetheless consonant with what he has already said. This seems to me strange, for, if 'the person himself' is 'a simple mental continuant', how is it possible to say more about what it is in itself beyond the recognition of it by each one of us in his own case, and the ascription of the like to others. There is, of course, as I have shown, a problem of how we are certain that the person, as we all apprehend ourselves to be at any time, is the same as the one who experienced or did something else at another time, and I have indicated how we may think of this on the basis of memory in the strict sense and of events which we have reason to relate to this as a continuity of the experience of the same being. It is also possible to use the word 'person' differently; that is, rather than identify 'the person himself', as Mr Foster does initially, firmly with 'the subject of consciousness', we may think of person as the totality to which both physical and mental properties are ascribed; and, at one point, Mr Foster declares that, although the person is 'essentially mental and only contingently corporeal', we also find ourselves 'qualifying for personhood only in virtue of this combining of body and mind'. The concept of a person becomes thus 'a subject of both mental and physical attributes', 'to be analysed in terms of the special way in which two logically separable components, a body and a mind, combine'.[55]

If this were a matter of words, it need not trouble us greatly, and perhaps not at all. It is perfectly proper to ask questions about the relation of the mind to the body and how we can best understand the relation of the two in the continuity of their very close combination in any particular case. But this is a further and distinct problem, and it is bound to be a little misleading to set it out as an account of persons if a person is also affirmed to be 'essentially mental'. I suspect that Mr Foster has brought some confusion into his own thinking in this way. He has tried to answer the further problem as if, in the last resort the two problems were the same, and in this way he makes it hard for us to see how he can continue to maintain his thesis of a 'pure ego' and simple continuant — or take the full force and implications of this particular stance.

To carry out his task in more detail, Mr Foster calls upon David Hume to provide a supplementation, and, in this way, a corrective also of Descartes, the two becoming for once, rather strange and unexpected bedfellows. But first there has to be a radical corrective of Hume. 'We can, it seems, only make sense of a thought, perception or belief as the state of something which thinks, perceives or believes, and this intelligibility seems to evaporate if the *something* is equated with, or dissolved into, a collection of discrete items'.[56] The something in question is not 'a conceptual illusion sustained by dispensable features of our mental language',[57] but is rather to be found in 'our introspective awareness'.[58] On the other hand, we have to make sense of the concept of a continuing subject and this involves giving an account of 'the continuity between successive phases of the same subject';[59] and the only way to do this, since time and not physical location is 'the only dimension' here, is in terms of 'unifying relations between mental items'.[60] This is where Hume is so helpful, the Cartesian making the mistake of grounding 'the unity of the mind wholly on the identity of the subject'.[61]

Locke had come close to this, combining a Cartesian acceptance of mental substance with a Humean view of subject identity, but he also got the worst of both views by failing to take the identity of the substance to be the same as the identity of the subject to whom mental states 'are ascribable in the ordinary sense'.[62] What we have to do, on the contrary, is 'to construe the subject as a simple and genuine mental continuant, but explain its identity in terms of unifying relations between its states'.[63]

This is a bold, but, it seems to me, misconceived enterprise. If the subject is 'a simple mental continuant', I do not see how its identity can also consist of relations between its states. The latter, on a Cartesian view, can only disclose to us the particular modes of the continuity of the subject in its various experiences, according to what these happen to be. It does not tell us at all what the nature of the subject — and its unity — is in itself. Indeed if we proceed by way of the unity of the relations, it is hard to see how we could ever get beyond them.

In his own account of the requisite unity of our mental states Mr Foster turns attention mainly to sense experience, interpreted broadly to cover hallucinations, bodily sensations and mental imagings, to 'explain the identity of a subject in terms of actual and potential sensible continuity among items in that domain'.[64] The key idea here is a special interlocking of presentations made possible when there is an overlap of some last portion of a successive total presentation with the first portion of another — 'in other words, a presentation of a temporal pattern is itself temporarily extended, and it overlaps its predecessor and successor in, so to speak, presentational substance to the extent that its pattern overlaps theirs in phenomenal content. It is this double overlap which provides the sensible continuity of sense experience and unifies presentations into a stream of awareness'.[65] There is a 'projection through time of the unity of a presentation' and this makes possible the projection through time of the individuality of the subject 'at a moment' and thus his persistence by 'the overlapping of his successive total presentations, the same awareness being preserved, as it were, through a constant contraction and expansion at its temporal edges'.[66]

This is a little reminiscent of the much discussed 'specious present', but it is not quite the same notion. It is deployed, within the limits of one paper, with great ingenuity and skill, and it may well have great importance for our understanding of perceptual awareness. This is not the place to consider it closely on its own account in that context. My own complaint is with the submission that, if this analysis or any amplification of it is sound, it is here 'in the unity of a stream that we primarily discern the identity of a subject'.[67] Even when we extend, as Mr Foster does, the unity found in a single stream to sets of streams, we are still in the realm of the contiguity and overlap of the mental states or experiences themselves, and, once we have made this the proper provenance for our discussion, the talk of a pure ego and simple continuant sounds rather strange. The considerations adduced by Mr Foster may provide grounds for positing a continuing subject, along the lines of Kant, but even that seems a little remote from the 'something' that is reflected in introspective awareness. If the identity of the subject is equated with the kind of identity established, along the lines indicated, then it would seem that the insistence on the simple and essentially mental continuant, 'the subject of consciousness', has been defeated by the mistaken supposition that the identity and nature of this kind of subject can be explained, and requires to be explained, in some further terms. What Mr Foster seems to be offering us at the start, and of which he seems very firmly convinced, becomes, in its translation from a Cartesian to a Humean guise, a very different sort of creature altogether; and is not the moral of this that we must not be faint-hearted if clear reflection presents us, at some points in our thinking, with something which has to be taken in the immediacy and finality in which it presents itself to us and without the explanation of what it is in itself which can only explain away?

This becomes peculiarly evident in the closing stages of Mr Foster's discussion. For he believes that we can not only find the individuation of the subject 'in the overlapping of his successive total presentations',[68] but that we can, indeed that we must, give a further account for the extension to sets of streams of the kind of unity found in a single stream; and while this may be taken to be 'logically grounded on the continuity of the subject',[69] there is 'an alternative and attractive explanation' in terms of 'certain natural laws' which involve 'dependence on the same brain'. If this merely means that we must, in a Kantian way, insist that awareness of persistent subjectivity requires a unified or ordered experience and that, for us, this involves an ordered physical reality and one's own brain, there would be nothing to be seriously disputed. But in what sense are these supplementary considerations thought to be attractive *alternatives*? Do they in themselves relate at all directly to the unity of the subject? Mr Foster does allow (as indeed he seemed earlier to insist) that 'a logically possible alternative would be a persistence relation of a purely mental kind' although he 'cannot think of any empirically plausible example'.[70] But the position in which he seems to come to rest at the close is that 'the persistence of a subject is the persistence of a capacity' which thus stretches 'across periods of unconsciousness by a law-based potential',[71] the latter in turn depending on the brain; and there is the possibility in this way also of 'splitting and fusing', of two subjects, 'for a certain period' sharing 'numerically the same mental states'. This is not, it is admitted, 'as radically dualistic' as Descartes' doctrine. But have we not at this point departed altogether from Descartes? Mr Foster states that he has 'to recognise the possibility of subjects who are self-sufficient in Descartes's way'[72] but he is 'not committed to saying that *all* subjects are of that sort, nor, in particular, that *we* are'.[73] It might be thought possible to have some disembodiment by 'a severing of the neural connections between brain and body', but 'our existence is dependent on the existence of our brains and on these laws, (1) and (2), whereby the same brain sustains the same awareness'.[74]

If this merely meant that, in the experience and existence we find that we have, we are in fact embodied and extensively dependent on our brains, nobody need seriously quarrel with it. We are clearly dependent, in point of fact, on our brains at the moment. But Mr Foster seems to be suggesting also that this is inherently unavoidable for us, that no other sort of embodment or of intelligible experience is even conceivable for us, and this (which makes it very much worse in my view) is because Mr Foster favours a view of the very nature of the subject itself, the 'attractive alternative', in terms of capacities and laws made possible by our brains, in other words making us *essentially* dependent on our brains and perhaps, in the last resort, identical with them; and however much this may allow us to retain the Cartesian terminology of 'the simple mental continuant' etc., this seems now peculiarly far removed from the 'subject of consciousness' 'reflected in the nature of our introspective awareness' and 'the subject of physical states only through his contingent attachment to a particular body'.

I hope I am not doing Mr Foster an injustice, and I come to my conclusion with some reluctance in view of Mr Foster's firm repudiation of Professor Strawson's 'co-ascription of mental and physical attributes to the same subject', but I find it hard all the same to avoid concluding that Mr Foster, though initially convinced of the distinctively mental nature of the 'simple continuant' disclosed in introspective awareness — and being thus very close at least to what Descartes maintained — has found it hard to break away as firmly as he seemed to do from the prevailing corporealist doctrines of the self and has set out to reconcile two positions which seem to be as radically opposed to one another as any philosophical positions could be. He sets out running well with the Cartesian hounds but is found in due course to be running also, not only with Humean hares but also with 'corporealist' ones; and I do not think that any amount of ingenuity can make this a sensible course to take.

8 Shifts of Emphasis

We have seen earlier, in Chapter 6, how some writers sought the answer to the problem of personal identity, or at least to what matters when we are concerned about our own identity and persistence, in various features of our characters or the course of the kind of experience we have. This was thought to do justice to the insights and sensitivity we have in being concerned about our own future or 'abiding' existence. But there are also writers of today who, without being much concerned about any insights to be salvaged from the traditional view, direct our attention entirely to the identity of persons in the empirical or phenomenalist sense. By this shift of emphasis, the claims of the more traditional view of the self, as a strict subject of experience, are not so much rebutted as abandoned in favour of a different issue, although one that is also of great importance in itself. This leaves the impression that all that matters has been fairly investigated.

This procedure is made more attractive because it has also some affinities (in the prominence accorded to memory for example) with the view I have commended earlier. But however illuminating in these ways, the impression is left that the case for the Platonic-Cartesian view, as it is commonly named today, has been not so much reckoned with as disregarded, or thrust out of the picture as of no importance, in the concentration on very different aspects of the problem as a whole.

I turn now to two examples of this particular shift of emphasis. The first is a further paper in the volume of essays in honour of Sir Alfred Ayer. It is by Professor Richard Wollheim and entitled 'Memory, Experiential Memory and Personal Identity'.

Professor Wollheim stays firmly with the declaration that 'whatever else personal identity resides in, it does not reside in a continuing unchanging substance'.[1] This, he thinks, 'was brilliantly enunciated by Hume'. But in presenting, in this context, his own account of personal identity, Professor Wollheim accords a central place to memory, as I do, though it is not always clear to me whether memory is invoked, in this case, as an account of what makes us persons or as a criterion by which we establish our continuity from one state of mind to another.

On the view I have advanced, we know what it is essentially to be a person from the way each one knows himself, in his own case, to be the person he is. Memory is not constitutive of what we are, nor of our continuity over a period of time. But it does provide us with the firmest assurance, in the case of strict memory, of our being the same persons now and in some previous experiences. It seems however that for Professor Wollheim this sort of distinction is not sharply drawn and that it is memory that in fact makes us the continuing and developing persons that we are.

One of Professor Wollheim's procedures is to dissociate himself very sharply from the view of Professor Ayer who continues to think of memory as essentially cognitive. It is not primarily cognitive for Wollheim, and indeed it is not clear that it is cognitive at all. The important feature of memory, for any account we have to give of personal identity, is certainly not for him a cognitive one. But the most that he explicitly says is that the cognitive view of memory is 'inadequate at least for one type of memory — and that, in the present context, the all-important type'.[2]

I find it very odd that the cognitive feature of memory should be played down in this way. Even if it is wrong to think of memory, as Professor Ayer rightly is thought to hold, as 'through and through cognitive', it is in its cognitive aspect that we normally think of it, and it is in that way that it is usually invoked as having prime importance in a sound account of our awareness of our own continuity. To remember something is to become aware, in some fashion whatever that may be, of something that happened and which we have experienced earlier ourselves, to be assured of what was the case on some earlier occasion. This makes memory, if not cognitive through and through, at least primarily and centrally cognitive.

The main account of memory which Professor Wollheim offers us is a causal one. I have always been a little perplexed as to what a causal account of memory would involve if we think of memory, as I think we should, as essentially or primarily cognitive. There are, of course, causal factors in our having memories, as there are of any other state of mind. These will not be exhaustively states of our bodies. The nature of thought itself has its part to play, as I have stressed earlier. But if the body, and especially the brain, begins to fail or is damaged, then our ability to remember is apt to be impaired, sometimes very seriously. It is for reasons such as these that it is sometimes said that our memories are stored in our brains, and provided that we realise that this is a very metaphorical way of speaking, there is no harm in it. But our memories are not strictly stored. They are either live occasions of recalling the past, or, in the less strict sense, bringing to mind what we have come to know in some other way, as when we remember some event we have been told about or discovered for ourselves — or the memory may be the dispositional proclivity or capacity to recall in those ways. Neither of these are things which can properly be thought to be stored. The brain, whatever else it is, is not a receptacle in which memories, least of all live states of mind, are stored or housed like birds in the aviary. But subject to this caution, we can very properly maintain that there are causal conditions of our being able to remember, and that states of our brains, and of our bodies generally as affecting these, have a very important place among such conditions.

It is for the physiologist, and especially those who concentrate on study of the brain, to tell how precisely the brain functions in memory. But there is no difference in principle here from the case of other states of mind. It may turn out to be easier in actual fact to ascertain what part or what functioning of the brain is involved in memory, by contrast, for example, with more ratiocinative processes. But in all the experiences we normally have there are bodily conditions, and especially states of the brain, which are substantially involved in our having the sort of experiences we do have. The part which the body plays in perception, for example, is peculiarly evident, however much it needs the expert to tell the story in its fullness.

But however much we may have to take account of physiological processes in considering how we come to have the experiences we do have, it would be quite wrong to suppose that this causal story builds up into an analysis or description of what it is to have those experiences or of what they are in themselves. We do not, even in perception, give a causal account of what it is to see and hear, we only indicate certain conditions of our being able to see and hear, conditions which may, or may not, be thought to be indispensable. There is a sense in which the stimulation of my eye by an external object, and thereby the stimulation of my brain, brings about the seeing which ensues upon the change in my brain. But the dependence remains a contingent one, and we are even told of plausible cases, like out-of-the-body experiences, where the normal causal processes seem not to be operative. There is no proper explanation of what it is to see in noting the physiological factors which normally bring this about.

This, it seems to me, holds of all states of mind. We may give an account of the causal factors involved, but it would be odd to regard this as offering a causal theory of our states of mind. This seems to me peculiarly true of memory. To indicate the physiological factors involved does not tell us what memory in itself is. This is true whether we think of memory in a dispositional way or as the actual recall of what we have learnt or come to know. It is more obviously the case when we think of live or, as I have called it, strict instances of remembering, as when I remember having my breakfast this morning. I could not, in any normal expectation, do this, if certain things were wrong with my brain, as happens in senility. But this does not tell us properly what it is to remember or why we can put reliance, as we normally do, on such remembering. These are the major philosophical issues about memory, and they are little affected by the account we give of the physiological factors involved. If, therefore, a causal theory of memory involves simply making us aware of the part which our bodies, and especially our brains, play in our being able to remember, there can be no serious objection to it. But it would be very misleading, on that account, to claim to be offering a causal theory of what it is to remember and of the other central philosophical questions involved, such as the reliance we place on our memories. I am quite foxed to know what it would be to offer a causal theory of memory in these central philosophical respects.

This is especially true when we think of memory, as we normally do, as a way of bringing to mind with assurance certain events which we experienced, or in which we participated in the past, that is when we take memory to be primarily, if not necessarily, cognitive. But perhaps something is involved here, in the alleged causal theory, other than the causal physiological factors. It could be truly said that I could not strictly remember having my breakfast this morning, if the latter had not in fact occurred, any more than I can be thought to perceive a table if there is no table in the room where I seem to see one. The presence of the table, whatever our theory of external objects, is a prerequisite of my seeing it. But it would be very odd to say, for this reason, that the table causes me to see it. In the same way, it would be odd to say that my eating my breakfast this morning causes me to remember eating my breakfast if all that is involved in this is that I could not remember eating my breakfast if I had not in fact done so. It is only in a very trivial sense that eating my breakfast causes me to remember doing so. But in what other sense could it be maintained that my eating my breakfast causes or brings about my remembering just that. In short, if we think of memory in its proper cognitive sense, what sense that is not tautological could there be in offering a causal account of memory other than noting the causal physiological factors involved?

Professor Wollheim does not, however, have to answer these questions. For it is not with memory in its cognitive form, even if he does grant that there is such memory, that he is concerned. His concern is with memory in its 'affective' form. By this he understands the following. The events which we experience, and indeed those of which we come to know in other ways, make some impact upon us, sometimes slight and sometimes considerable; and this may enter into our dispositional attitudes and proclivities in various ways. This provides for him the basis for a causal view of memory and the way it matters in personal identity. This takes us well beyond the 'empiricist' view of memory as simply a relation holding between experiences. This latter 'parsimonious' view of memory must be replaced by the notion of memory as a capacity and of persons as the means 'to house such a disposition'.

The deployment of this view is undertaken in considerable detail and with much subtlety. I shall not attempt to follow the details of Professor Wollheim's analysis. The main consideration centres on what he calls 'experiential memory'. This is contrasted with both 'recollection' and 'retention'. In the first of these latter two we come to know the original event at second hand, for example by hearing or reading about it. In the second case we first learned about the event at first hand, by ourselves seeing or hearing it for instance. In 'experiential memory' we came to know of the event 'from the inside' in 'the performance of it, or the suffering of it, knowingly'.

It is in terms of those distinctions that we must account for what is called here 'the Goethe case', that is the situation when we are not quite certain that we remember something because we have been told about it or because we were ourselves involved at the time, that is remember it in what I have earlier myself called 'the strict sense'. The 'acquisition condition' is different in the two cases instanced. When we realise in due course that we do strictly remember, 'we should explain this switch by invoking a change in the relative causal efficacies of the reasons related to the different types of memory'.[3]

What is of main importance is that, in the case of 'experiential memory' taken to have much in common with 'central imagining', as the author elsewhere describes that, 'it is not the case that the satisfier of the acquisition condition is a cognitive state — if this is taken to mean a purely cognitive state'.[4] 'Experiential memory has a distinctive phenomenology'.[5] This means that 'I *shall tend* to remember, both systematically and liberally, what I thought and what I felt'[6] in the initial doing or suffering at the time; and, in addition, 'I shall tend to rethink or refeel those very thoughts and feelings'; the initial state or condition will tend 'to set itself up afresh in the mind'.[7] This is 'the "affective tendency" of experiential memory' and 'the state or condition that results' is 'the "affective tone" of experiential memory'.[8] The latter is not just an accompaniment to the phenomenon, 'it also shows how the causal history that we assign to experiential memory must differ in an overall way from the causal histories we assign to other types of memory', it must be the sort that can 'explain the affective tendency in experiential memory'.[9] We not only come to know the initial event *'from the inside'* but also find ourselves *'experiencing it from the inside'*,[10] or finding that it modifies 'at one and the same time the cognitive store and the affective store of the person whose state it was'.[11]

In fairness, we have to entertain at this point the possibility that 'the affective influence of an event (could) be exerted across persons';[12] and in one sense this seems quite sensible. The 'affective tone' of an event, as it figures in my own attitudes etc., could be conveyed to others and help to determine their attitudes. But this, on the other hand, only becomes possible through various ways in which we convey, deliberately or otherwise, our own situation to others. There is no direct influence of the initial event on the attitudes and capacities of others. This is why, although starting with an open mind so as not to beg the question in days when fission and fusion are seriously entertained in fashionable philosophy, Professor Wollheim is forced to conclude that, while 'an event can exert an affective influence through experiential memory', that itself 'could not initiate the exercise of such an influence across persons', for 'the affective tone itself attests to an affective influence already exerted over the person by the event'.[13] 'The original affective influence of an event upon him must be *that at the time of the event*, or what I shall call "the contemporaneous affective store"'.[14]

The function of memory comes to be thought of in this way as putting us 'under the influence of a particular piece of the past',[15] as this was perceived (recollection) or 'as this was experienced' (experiential memory). This is why such memory can have therapeutic value, we relive some piece of the past and appreciate some ways in which we succeeded or failed to cope with it. This links us still more closely to the initial event and is thus 'another reason for thinking that experiential memory cannot run across persons'.[16]

It is in these ways that all of us 'can develop into the persons that we become'. And if the deep effect of thus 'looking out over life' seems strange 'we must reflect that we respond not only to the colours and the contours of the scene but also to the feelings and emotions that these familiar objects arouse within us'.[17] And thus, by abandoning the purely cognitive view we arrive at 'a truly explanatory account of human identity. At the core of the account is this insight: *if experiential memory is criterial of person identity, it is so just because it is also creative of personal identity*. In experiential memory the past affects us in such a way that we become creatures with a past: creatures, that is, tied to the past in the way peculiar to persons'.[18]

There is much besides this in the details of Professor Wollheim's discussions, his account of 'screen memory', for instance, and the distinction between ways in which these may be branches of a memory path and branches off a memory path, as this bears on questions of fusion and fission; but the central contention which concerns us now is the one just made, namely that our identity turns especially on the way our reactions to various particular events are perpetuated and extended in 'the reinforcement of the original impact by later experiential memory of the event',[19] the expansion and mediation of the past in present attitudes being made possible by the original impact of the event, as this 'accrues' to experiential memory. This is the causal way in which memory ensures our identity from one situation to another, this memory is constitutive in the way it makes us what we are in essential linkage with our past.

I have little doubt that an analysis along these lines is of great importance for our understanding of ourselves and our identity at *a certain level*, whether or not we follow Professor Wollheim in all the details of his account. But it is still a matter of operating only *at one level*, the level of what I set forth above as the self in the sense in which it may be described. We are still concerned with the psychology and phenomenology of the self, with the way I am and become the sort of person which my life has made me, with the continuity of my past in the shaping of my dispositions and character. The more insight we have into this process the better, but there remain very different questions which cannot be answered in these ways, questions which, moreover, thrust themselves upon us even within the limited scope of the phenomenological study itself. For we have still to ask how the present reaction to some event does in fact perpetuate itself in some capacity or attitude which it makes possible. It may be wrong to suppose that these attitudes continue by inhering in some quasi-physical substance. But neither can we leave them high and dry in some sublime isolation of their own or simply subject to some peculiar mechanism of their own blending and inter-relatedness. There may not be anything we can say about a disposition and its changes and development as such, and we are all anxious today not to hypostatise abstractions. It nontheless seems unsatisfactory simply to note our dispositions and tell the story of them. There must be something further which ensures this.

But what can this something further be other than the same consciousness continuing in the awareness of being the consciousness it is and sustaining the influence of its past because it is the same consciousness. I very much stressed above the peculiar involvement of the self, as the ultimate subject of experience, with the course of its own experience and the development or other changes in our dispositional make-up. The self, I stressed, is not just appended to character and experience. It is involved in them, and this makes it possible for us sometimes to lose sight of the ultimate self altogether, we cannot find it as a thing apart. It is nonetheless apprehended by each one in his own case as that without which neither experience nor disposition could have significance. To drop it out of sight, in the story we tell about ourselves in terms of experience and character, is to forfeit everything which makes that story itself possible and significant.

Even if this were not the case, we should hardly come to that conclusion simply on the basis of effectively telling the story of our identity in the describable form of experience and character. The question has at least to be raised of whether there is not some more fundamental sense of our own identity, and how this must be conceived. We do not answer this question, but simply pass it by in our concentration on how experience continues and character shapes itself. Professor Wollheim may be right in his rejection of some idea of an unchanging substance. But he does nothing to substantiate this by the effectiveness of his dealing with another question. In short, the issue as between Hume and Kant or Descartes cannot be wished away in terms of an answer to a quite different question. It must be faced on its own account, whichever side we take. Professor Wollheim is simply not addressing himself to the question of self-identity in the form in which that question has been most fundamentally a question with which philosophers have peculiarly concerned themselves. We cannot turn to phenomenology, however impressive, for an answer to an essentially philosophical question.

The same tendency to raise, or seem to raise, one sort of question and proceed to answer in terms of another question, is even more marked in the work of some other writers of today. I turn now to a further example, a much more patent one than Professor Wollheim.

In his address to the Joint Session of the Mind Association and the Aristotelian Society at Swansea, the late Professor J. R. Jones begins with a firm and very sharp contrast of his own position with my own. He thought it was 'senseless' to suppose that one could assign experiences to an identified owner 'by simply consulting' one's experiences directly. For this would imply, he thought, 'that I inwardly scan a number of *different* consciousnesses'.[20] I would be picking out my own experiences as my own in the same way as I would pick my umbrella from a stand or my hat from a peg. There would have to be some peculiarity of the umbrella, its location at least and almost certainly much besides, to distinguish it from the others.

This submission made by Professor Jones is not so common today as it used to be, and it will be evident already how I respond to it. I do indeed know *other* minds on evidence of some sort, even in the case of telepathy, if it happens. But what evidence could I seek for my certainty that I am now in pain (if I were so) and that it is me who is in pain, or that I am having now these thoughts that I put on paper, and that it is myself who is thinking them, even if others think along similar lines? All this has been stressed already. Professor Jones made two further moves that I wish to note.

In the first place he had recourse to the now familiar ploy in Wittgensteinian philosophy, namely to maintain that where there is no doubt, or a possibility of error, there can be no point in claiming to know. As Professor Jones himself puts it, 'there can be no ascribing to an identified subject where there is no question of mis-ascribing'.[21] I have never understood the appeal of this procedure. If it is a matter of legislating about the use of the word 'know', then it may not be as serious as it seems. But since the word 'know' is also being used in the way we would normally use it, I fail altogether to understand why we cannot be said to know simply because the issue is not in doubt. It may be peculiarly pointless in practice to affirm vigorously, or indeed at all, something that is evident beyond any question; but, if anything, that would seem also to make it exceptionally clear that what is pointless to affirm, in this way, is so because it is so evidently the case and true. The claim of truth is strengthened, not weakened, in such instances. There may be no point in insisting that the pain I feel is mine, but this does not preclude me from being firmly convinced that it is so.

The matter might be different if I could form no opinion as to what it would be like for my belief to be false, but, when I affirm that I am in pain, there is no difficulty at all in understanding what it would be like for this not to be true, namely my being comfortable or not in pain. Likewise, there is no problem about understanding what it would be like for it to be someone else and not me in pain. None of this is questioned when it is claimed, in self-ascription, that it is beyond any possible doubt for me that the pain is mine. How could I have an actual pain, and not just a possible source of pain, without being certain that I had it, and what could be more inane, in this case, than to begin to wonder whether after all it may not be someone else?

But how is this to be understood if it is also the case, as Professor Jones maintains, that 'my avowals are not self-ascriptions',[22] if, that is, in having no possible doubt about being in pain, I am, nevertheless, not ascribing this pain to an identifiable owner or subject. On the latter score there is no concession, it being further stressed, in relation to the view that memory might be a criterion of self-identity, that, whatever may be said about memories, 'they are not memories of past "episodes of consciousness", whatever that might mean'.[23] I find Professor Jones's puzzlement here very strange. It is quite true that my memories are, usually at least, memories of *'situations* in which this person became involved'.[24] I say 'usually', as I am not certain what we should say here when we remember a dream, or even a train of thought or rumination. There is obviously some sort of situation in a dream, or in most dreams. When I dream that I am playing tennis, there is much common to this and actually playing, the court where I seem to be playing, the balls, the rackets, my companions etc. There is also the actual state of my body in bed, but that is not what I remember when I recall my dream, nor are the court and the rackets and my friends, in this case, other than items in my own consciousness in my dream, even if I am dreaming about a real court and real people. When I am, by contrast with dreams, just absorbed in my own thinking, it is not likely that I shall be wholly oblivious of the world around me, but what I remember especially is the course of my own thinking.

Even in situations which have clearly their outward or physical components and other real people, as when I remember having my breakfast this morning, a great deal of what I remember is what I myself was thinking or intending — how amused I was by someone's remark, the choices I made from the menu, being pleased or displeased at what was set before me, my perception of the room or enjoyment of the bright sunshine outside or concern about getting wet later if it is raining hard, or the course of an argument I had. I was aware all the time I was having my breakfast, I was not eating like a machine sucking something into its maw. It seems to me therefore clear that part of what I remember, in this and like instances, is certainly my own states of consciousness at the time, and I am quite at a loss to understand why this should be thought to be so preposterous.

But if there can be no ascribing of states of mind, or 'episodes of consciousness', to a subject at a particular time, and to the same subject at various times, if 'I have', in avowals of pain and the like, 'does not express assignation to an identified owner'[25] and there can thus, in the quotation made with approval from Wittgenstein, be 'no question of recognising a person when I say

"I have toothache"',[26] what alternative account can we offer in these situations? What is the proper force of 'I have' here and of '*my* pain', and of the absurdity of seeking some evidence for making such avowals? What are we doing in such cases that seems beyond all disputation?

The answer to this is given in terms of the notion of 'there being the world which *death* will end'.[27] This is a 'neighbourless world', and what my pain-avowal communicates is 'the neighbourless fact that a pain is currently involved in there being the world which will stop existing when I die. Asking how I *know* I have a toothache is asking *how I know this fact*, and *that* is what is nonsensical'.[28] But have we got rid of the domination of the possessive here, have we guarded sufficiently against the 'intrusion of possessor-level grammar'? What is this world that ends with my death? It is clearly not what we ordinarily mean by 'the world'. It would be an 'intolerable paradox' to say that anyone's death will end the world in that sense. The world will still go on. What sort of a world then will come to an end? Can we avoid saying, 'the world of *my* experiences', or 'the world as I see it', or some variation on this? *My* world will come to an end, but now we are back again with the embarrassing possessive which we are trying to exclude. What is the purport of 'my' in such a context?

At this point recourse is had to a distinction which Wittgenstein had drawn between two 'levels of grammatical language'. At one of these, the use of 'I' is on the same grammatical level as the use of 'he' or 'other people', and, at this level, it is replaceable by 'this body'. At this level, Jones insists, I am picked out simply as 'a certain occupant of space'. I know myself, at this level, simply as 'a space-occupant'. I seem also, however, to be more than this, but certainly not 'a bodiless subject'. The latter supposition is conclusively refuted, it is thought, in Professor Strawson's insistence that I ascribe predicates to myself in the same way as, by observation, I ascribe them to others. In the ascription of experiences I am on the same level as other people, and Strawson's account of the primitiveness of the concept of a person is thought to provide 'substantial corroboration' of the view that, if there is self-ascription at all, it must be to me as a body, 'a space-occupant'. But there remains a 'disquietude' about this. Everything has not been said. There is some '*radical* asymmetry'[29] in the ascriptions to oneself rather than others, and Strawson does not allow for this, he leaves it 'prematurely blocked'.[30]

At the second level I am, as Wittgenstein had put it, 'without neighbours' and cannot therefore identify myself', 'there could be no question of my knowing who I am'.[31] but that is not all. For there is also, as noted 'the world that will end with my death'. Little is said to indicate precisely how this is to be understood. It is apparently a world of experiences and, to that extent, not just a bodily world. But even this is unclear, for everything seems to be reduced, at this stage, 'simply to "the world's being there"'.[32] 'Wittgenstein contrasts "consciousness physiologically understood or understood from outside" with "consciousness as the very essence of experience, the appearance of the world, the world"'.[33] In my view 'the world's being there' is not enough to cover my apprehension of the world. I do not normally pause to take note of this apprehension. All the same, the mere fact of the book's being on the table is not the same as my perceiving it. I do not, even on a Berkeleyan view, just perceive a state of my mind. There is, moreover, much in the world which we never apprehend. It is also very hard to understand what is meant by 'consciousness physiologically understood' or 'all experience is world'.

Undaunted by any perplexity here, Professor Jones, staying very closely with Wittgenstein, insists boldly that, when I am not being identified as a body, 'I also no longer know who I am. For there being the world is now all that the use of "I" succeeds in expressing. And there being the *world* in a sense covers everything. This makes "I" at this level co-extensive with everything'.[34] It 'shrinks', as Wittgenstein had put it, 'to a point without extension, and there remains the reality co-ordinate with it'.[35] 'You cannot know who you are at a level where you are simply reduced to "everything's being there"'.[36] But, even so, there remains some sense in which we are to refer to the world that ends with *my* death. My pain is mine simply in the sense of occurring at some point in this world. But now we have the further move of referring us back to the other level, the one at which I 'have neighbours' and can be identified as one body among others, and having the pain is just 'one of the experiences of this space-occupant. That is what makes it "*my* pain"'.[37]

The really serious problems seem to elude us entirely in these curious moves. We cannot be quite certain that what is being offered is straightforward corporealism, but what there is beyond this remains most obscure, even experiences being equated with 'the world's being there'. The most that we have is an alleged new grammatical level; and in that case it is hard to understand the significance of singling out the events that begin with my body being animate and end with my drawing the last breath or whatever the clinical criterion of bodily death may be. Why select this particular series of events and why attach importance to the pain as mine simply because it is one of these? Where there is no recognition that experience itself is not physical, it is not strange that the question of experiences being had by a person appears to be pointless. One wonders why so much ingenuity should be wasted upon it.

One wonders also why the terminal point of the bodily series should have so much importance. Why not stay with the identification of persons, at the appropriate grammatical level if we must think in those terms, in a bodily way? How does the preoccupation with the ending of it at 'my death' come about? I suggest that behind all this concern there is more than the attempt to make a particular bodily series specific. There is a profoundly misleading conflation of two very different questions. Both of these concern some sense in which we may come to better understanding of ourselves or who we are. Let me make this plainer.

It is possible that the awareness of our own mortality, and having this reflectively in mind, may help us to a fuller understanding of the sort of persons we are and what may lie ahead for us. How far, if at all, this is true, I would not care to say. It has been thought to be true by notable persons like John Donne. But this is a quite different phenomenological (or, perhaps religious) issue that has nothing whatsoever to do directly with the question of self-identity in the form in which philosophers have been most concerned to examine it, the question at issue for instance between Hume and Kant. The fact that we will die appears to be totally irrelevant to this and would not usually be brought into the discussion.

Suppose, for example, we thought there were celestial beings, angels and archangels etc. We might or might not ascribe some quasi-physical form to these. As men in various cultures and religions have pictured them, they have some form of that kind, but whether they have or not we distinguish one from the other; and they themselves presumably, if they exist at all, distinguish themselves from one another. Michael would know that he is not Gabriel. All the same it has not usually been supposed that such superior beings would ever die. There may or may not be a reason for such beliefs. But the point is that the supposition that celestial beings were not mortal proved no obstacle to regarding them as distinct beings who would also be aware, in each case, of the difference between each and the others.

Suppose again, to come down to earth, we envisage a number of infants stranded on a solitary island, as older children were in *The Lord of the Flies*. Suppose they have lived a very sheltered life before that, and had never been told, or had anything in their lives to suggest, that their lives would end some day. They flourish and grow up on their island on a vegetarian diet and they never encounter the bodies of any dead creatures, not even dead fish being washed ashore. It may thus never occur to them that they would not go on for ever. But this would be no bar at all to their distinguishing one from the other. They would presumably remember their names or acquire the equivalent. One would be John and one would be Jane, and all this identification of who each of them was would proceed entirely without any thought of their eventual death. If they became sharp enough to reflect philosophically, they might wonder what all this involved; is it just a matter of their having different bodies, or is there more than this to each one being the one he is? If they cannot raise such questions themselves, we could certainly raise them on their behalf, and, I submit, we would do so on the basis of what seems at present the case about them, without any regard at all to the fact that they would die some day. The fact that we die, however fundamental in other contexts, in no way affects the question what makes a person, in virtue of what we find ourselves to be, the distinct person that he is.

The religious agnostic is not debarred from giving the same sort of answer to the initial question about self-identity as the religious person who has expectation of a future life. We may indeed take this further. Suppose one does believe in God. This is a belief in a spiritual, and usually personal, being, but also one who cannot be thought of as non-existing. He exists, it is usually thought, by the necessity of his own nature. We have to be cautious when we consider how our talk about such a being should be properly understood, and we must not be too anthropomorphic in conceiving of him. All the same it would be strange to say, as the

Wittgenstein represented in the above discussion would have to say, that God, who does not die, cannot, for that reason, have the faintest idea who he is.

9 Some Recent Continental Thinkers

I have been trying to show how easy it is to slide from one vital question about persons and their identity to another very different question, and thus very seriously confusing the issue. The first question, the one with which this book is mainly concerned, is the one reflected in the point at issue between Kant (and Descartes and others before him) and Hume, namely whether we can properly speak of a self or subject which is not to be accounted for in terms of the course of our experiences or some feature of our dispositional nature and the attitudes and stances they determine, or of mere bodily continuity. The other is the question how we are to think of ourselves, and how we may best come to know ourselves, in the sense of understanding what sort of person one is, what are our likes and dislikes and how we are likely to respond to various situations, and so forth. The first is the more metaphysical and logical question, the second more psychological or empirical in a broad sense, though none of these appellations should be applied narrowly.

It will be evident from all I have said already that these two questions, and the very radical difference between them, in no way imply that there are two selves. It is the same me who likes this or that and is also an abiding subject through various changes of disposition or experience. But to ask what we are like — who or what am I? — in the sense of considering what my inclinations or possible stances are like — am I a nice person or a spiteful one or bolder perhaps than might appear? — is a very different matter from asking whether I who have these likes etc. can also know myself as a distinct being over and above my likes and attitudes and not capable of being accounted for or described in any such terms at all. This distinction should be clear from all that has been said already.

When we concern ourselves with the second question, in the

order of my listing, we do find that there is a wide scope for our investigation, and very deep and important questions; there is a variety of approaches to the subject and of techniques for the pursuit of it, some more adequate than others. We may approach it with some immediate purpose in hand, as a counsellor or a priest or in personal self-searching, or we may be more concerned with some general principles involved and the methods of study. Are we the sort of creatures that Thrasymachus or Hobbes envisaged or have we some genuine benevolence and concern for others? Are Freudian views about our motivations sound ones, do they need modification? Are the social sciences good guides to what human nature is like? How far can we deceive ourselves about what we are like, in general or in particular cases? How true is it that there are depths in our natures that are not evident on the surface, and how may they be plumbed? What limits and perils are there in various ways of dealing with these issues?

These, and their like, are very important questions, but they are not the questions with which I am particularly concerned in this study. They will become important elsewhere. I have great respect for those who are most skilled in handling them, in theoretical and practical contexts alike. They have a very important place in our over-all view of ourselves and any concern we may have for whatever may be said in a final or comprehensive way about our own existence. But I do not wish to take this further now.

The question what we are like, in the sense I have just indicated, may however easily extend itself into a further question which concerns more the purpose or value of our existence. 'What is man?' may be taken in an evaluational sense. It is a famous Biblical question. Some may give it a very non-Biblical answer, indeed an outright materialist one; others may turn to bold speculation, sometimes more, sometimes less religious, about some destiny or fulfilment we may be expected to have, as individuals or a community. These are also important questions however we may answer them, with high expectations or a very limited horizon. But they are not strictly the same as the question what we are like, in the descriptive sense, and they may involve very wide-ranging issues affecting the scope and justification of speculative and religious enquiry. If 'What is man?' is to be considered in religious terms there are obviously many forms and styles of enquiry that come into it, including the nature of God and our knowledge of him. But we have to be careful here also not to conflate the phenomenological question of what we may more explicitly discover about ourselves, individually or collectively, at the level of normal description of what we are like, and the wider questions, so far as appropriate, of some destiny or further purpose our lives may have.

It may be that the latter questions have a bearing on the more initial descriptive question, and the way we deal with the latter may affect our investigation of the other. But they are different questions and, initially at least, they should not be conflated. If they are, that could be seriously to the detriment of both enquiries. There is much to be considered at its own level before we move to an over-all view, as I hope again to stress elsewhere.

But what I wish to emphasise mainly at the moment is that both the investigations I have just been noting, the phenomenological and the speculative one, including repercussions they may have on each other, need to be very carefully distinguished from the question to which I give philosophical priority, the basic or initial question about self-identity, namely whether there is a self which is not to be captured in the net of the descriptions which we may offer of ourselves, as groups or individuals, but is known as subject or agent to each one in the very process by which particular properties come to be initially ascribed. The question whether there is, in the traditional meaning, a 'pure self' must be considered on its own account without contamination by other important questions we may ask about ourselves and without prejudice to the place such questions may have, and their relevance to one another, in any final or over-all view we may try to reach.

It must be added now that, in both sets of questions which I have distinguished from the question of the distinct subject of experience, there are many ways in which we may find our existence mysterious and elusive. The talk of mystery and an 'elusive' self is not inappropriate here. Quite obviously there is much mystery about our existence if we think of it in religious terms, but even at a more mundane level we may find ourselves much baffled or at a loss how to discover or apprehend various depths or complexities of our own natures. It may be that it is only in certain contexts that we may come to be properly known in this way. The danger is, however, that because we may very sensibly and fittingly speak of ourselves as elusive or mysterious to ourselves or others at this level, the invocation of this may be thought to be an adequate recognition of the essential elusiveness of persons in the more radical sense with which I have been concerned in preceding chapters. The case for Descartes and his like may go by the board in this way, or the impression may be created that what is at stake has been handsomely conceded, that the 'I' in all its essential elusiveness and the problems of providing an adequate description of it, has been fully taken into account and the course set for placing it in the more complete context of any final philosophical view we may seek.

I have set this out very fully, although much of it may be evident from what has been said already, because as soon as we move from the more explicitly professional handling of the subject, the confusions, already apt to bedevil the subject, as we have seen, even in strictly professional treatment, become more pronounced and a good deal more disastrous in their total effect.

This can be seen very clearly if we turn now to the work of some highly regarded and very influential Continental thinkers of today. Many of these, especially the phenomenologists and the existentialists, have brought the idea of the self into particular prominence in their own writings and have made it, in that way, a central theme for a great deal of recent theology as well as philosophy. The pre-eminence of Husserl here will be evident to most students of the subject, and it may be noted also how closely, in some respects, my own views follow the lines of his teaching. Indeed, the centrality of the subject itself is as plain in Anglo-Saxon and American philosophy, even in analytic and empiricist schools, as anywhere else; and it is regrettably overlooked what distinctive contributions have been made to the subject by outstanding English and American writers in a more speculative and less restrictive vein than the more fashionable forms of philosophical analysis, for example in the work of the thinkers noted already, H. J. Paton, C. A. Campbell and A. C. Ewing in Britain and Roderick Chisholm and Peter Bertocci (pre-eminent now in the 'Personalist' school of philosophy) in America. But it is to others, especially existentialists, that we owe mainly the centrality accorded extensively today to the inwardness of experience and the individual person at the core of it.

Such thinkers have also been the ones most concerned to relate the emphasis on inwardness to our other concerns and to what may be rather loosely described as our situation as a whole. It is, in this context at least, no accident that many such writers are men of letters as well as philosophers. The inwardness of persons, and the problems and complexities that arise in that way, is a dominant theme and preoccupation of novelists and other creative writers in our time, and this also, as again I hope to stress more elsewhere, is a very important pointer and guide to the way we must understand our place in an over-all view. But while the writers alluded to have the advantage in insightfulness and relevance, and also perhaps in forceful colourful writing, this virtue itself exposes them to sly temptation, they do not excel in ruthless analysis and, as Plato taught was so vital in philosophy, the drawing of distinctions which are significant and relevant as well as sound. For this reason we find them, most tantalisingly when our hearts warm to what they say, drifting from one important sense in which the elusiveness of the self and the inwardness of experience are effectively presented and stressed to a quite different extension of the same terms, and thereby very seriously blurring the very issues which they themselves have helped to bring to the forefront.

It would take disproportionate space in this book to survey the field in which the alleged confusions occur in any comprehensive way. A warning must suffice, but to reinforce the warning I shall refer to the work of three outstanding writers whose work, admittedly important, has been seriously marred and deprived of much of its effectiveness and relevance by little appreciated shifts of emphasis from one important theme to another masquerading as the first.

A significant, but impressive and cautious, precursor of much that we find today, in the context indicated, is the nineteenth-century philosopher, Wilhelm Dilthey. He was reacting especially against Neo-Kantian philosophers of his day, notably the Baden school, but had also in mind more severely empiricist thinkers such as J. S. Mill and others who came under a similar attack from their own idealist compatriots such as Green and Bradley. Dilthey draws a sharp distinction between the way we give a scientific account of the course of things in the world around us, and unify our impressions of it, and the understanding we have of our own experience and the course of our lives. 'The methods by means of which we study psychic life, history, and society are very different from those which have led to the knowledge of nature'.[1]

'Hypotheses do not all play the same role in psychology as in the study of nature'.[2] 'In the domain of psychic life, it is impossible to specify the facts with the exact determinacy which is required of a theory through the confrontation of its consequences with such data'.[3]

The main consideration here, and in many variations on the same theme, is 'the lived' character of 'the inner experiences themselves'. We have to heed what is 'continuously given as life itself'.[4] But we are also warned in the same context of the dangers of 'depending only on a subjective and equivocal psychology of life'.[5] As Professor Rudolf A. Makkreel observes, in his introduction to the same volume: 'The concept of lived experience is somewhat difficult to define and therefore has often been confused with that of inner experience ... Lived experience is broader in scope and certainly does not carry the subjective connotations so often associated with inner experience'.[6]

It is not altogether clear what is being rejected here, but the main emphasis is unambiguous. What Dilthey wants to bring into prominence is a peculiar unity of psychic existence which is given in all experience itself as an ineradicable feature of it. There is, as Professor Makkreel puts it again, 'an originally experienced sense of connectedness'.[7] There is, an essential 'psychic nexus' in all experience, 'an inner connectedness (*Zusammenhang*)' because psychic life is itself a nexus',[8] 'The human studies are distinguished from the sciences of nature first of all in that the latter have for their objects facts which are presented to consciousness as from outside, as phenomena and given in isolation, while the objects of the former are given originaliter from within as real and as a living continuum'.[9] It is this vital continuum that matters, and, by contrast with science, where a system of nature is established by 'inferential arguments which supplement the data of experience by means of a combination of hypotheses', in the human studies 'the nexus of psychic life constitutes originally a primitive and fundamental datum'.[10] The experienced (*erlebte*) whole (*Zusammenhang*) is primary here'.[11]

This is the proper 'psychological base' for human studies, and it enables us to avoid the dilemma of a purely subjective approach and also 'a superficial and sterile empiricism', an 'increasing separation of life from knowledge'.[12] No 'transcendental method', 'no legerdemain of the Kantian school'[13] will avail of itself, for the 'theoretician of knowledge' there presupposes and imports into his theory the 'nexus in his own living consciousness',[14] the 'unique nexus' which 'is originally and continuously given as life itself'.[15] There is no stage in which this is absent, but what is thus immanent in all experience can be made more explicit by reflection and understanding, the latter including in Dilthey's later thought much concern with expressions of experience and language. This has much to do with our knowledge of one another, and the initial disposition to regard our own inner experience as the intuitive basis for the understanding of others tends to give way to the more refined and objective understanding that comes through reflection on language and expression. This is not mere self-completion, nor, on the other hand, a self-transcendence involved in the concepts of objective expression and intentionality. The outer mode is taken up into the inner and reflected out again into our grasp of experience as a whole.

As Professor H. A. Hodges puts it: 'Thus lived experience and understanding, though theoretically separable, are in practice bound up with one another. We are present to ourselves in lived experience, but this experience needs to be clarified by understanding'.[16]

This understanding penetrates to 'mental attitudes (*Stellungen*) which lie deeper than the surface series of psychological events, and control it in the interests of wider purposes'.[17] The insights of our own lived experience provide the intuitive basis for the understanding of others, and to this extent the understanding of others is an extension of the initial experience of myself. Self-understanding is fundamental, but in later thought the emphasis is shifted by Dilthey to the greater role of understanding, with conscious reflection on the expressions of others. How far this shift goes is not clear, but it certainly does not seem to be a case of dispensing with the immediacy of the lived experience or superseding it. Even in our knowledge of others we need the insights of our knowledge of ourselves. Thus Hodges continues in the context from which I have quoted already: 'But further, the understanding of others would be essentially impossible, as a process, without the living movement and intimacy of lived experience ... Lived experience gives my experience reality and life, understanding gives it comprehensiveness and objectivity. The two are thus inseparable, and together form the basis of all our commerce with the world of the mind'.[18]

The question how far understanding may be thought to go

beyond *Erlebnis* or lived experience and to function independently in terms of reflection on language and expression is important
for my present purpose. But it is not as important as the question
of how we are to understand the initial continuum and nexus of
lived experience. Just what does the lived experience disclose to
us? One is disposed to assume that it gives us an immediate
awareness of our own mental processes, but the more we consider
the emphasis on inwardness and immediacy in the appropriate
contexts, the more it seems to be concerned with the nexus itself,
the continuum, the wholeness and comprehensiveness which is
initially evident, however incomplete, in the most elementary
and unreflective experience. Is there more than this initial and
self-developing unity, and just how must we understand that?

There clearly is more, but this itself seems to be conceived,
mainly if not wholly, in terms of the interplay of the strictly
cognitive features of experience with emotive and purposive
factors which are in turn deemed to be the essence of evaluation.
In the extension of Dilthey's initial themes to aesthetics and
historical understanding, with which he was especially concerned, it is this interplay that comes into prominence. And thus,
although Dilthey could not be thought to have fallen foul of 'the
philosophical breakers of Charybdis'[19] with the Neo-Kantians, in
seeking to avoid the reef of 'tedious empiricism' he does come a
little close to neglecting his own warning. It is some kind of
transcendental unity, some essential and peculiar wholeness, that
is most distinctively evident in the lived experience also and extended and made more explicit in understanding and reflection
on our expressions. It is this that is brought into prominence in
'adult psychic life'.[20]

The position is thus not so very far removed from that of more
typical nineteenth-century idealists, like the British philosophers
Green and Bradley and especially those, at the close of the pre-
eminence of idealism in British philosophy, who were concerned
to preserve a place for distinct persons as at least a special centre
of unification within the ultimate whole. How far this comparison
can go is not perhaps easy to settle, but it gains strength when we
find a drift also towards a more corporate doctrine of persons
than might be suggested initially in the prominence given to lived
experience and immediacy. There is 'a rediscovery of the I in the
Thou', and although this carries with it the insistence 'that the
individual is an intrinsic value', this is itself attenuated in the

notion of the individual as 'a structural configuration of certain dominant qualities'.[21] As Professor Makkreel puts it: 'The individuality of the self is defined in terms of the structural articulation of the acquired psychic nexus. No qualitative uniqueness need be posited to explain individuality'.[22] There is a sense indeed in which individuality ripens and is itself the goal of history. The individual is also thought of as a point of intersection of various cultural systems which have themselves 'a structural unity, comparable with that which we find in an individual'.[23]

It is not essential to understand this in a severely corporate sense, but it is also hard to see how that can be avoided when the individual, and his lived experience, is thought of mainly in terms of configurations of qualities and wholeness. The epistemological ego is certainly rejected, the concept of the self being 'explicated out of consciousness' and individuality 'defined through a psychic nexus that has been acquired'.[24] We can thus also 'speak of transpersonal subjects without reifying them'[25] and they can be 'logical carriers of objective spirit',[26] a *Zeitgeist*, though not the anthropormorphism of a *Volksseele*.

It is in these contexts that we see most clearly how the insistence on inwardness and an indispensable immediacy of experience can be given much prominence, and made fundamental, in very different contexts from those of the individual's immediate awareness of the course of his own experience and of himself as the irreducible subject of it. If there is a discovery of the self, and a mystery which remains, it is that of the proper placing of items of experience and the setting of our lives in a context which is not yet completely manifest to us. This is very different from the self-disclosure of immediate experience and the mysteriousness of the subject solely in the sense that it cannot be caught, in its essence, in descriptive characterisation.

It does not follow by any means that we must withhold from Dilthey the proper credit for all that he does say, although I suspect that he himself thought that he had said most, if not all, that it is important to say about the primacy and immediacy of lived experience. Others who came after him were certainly confused and assumed that, in setting our experiences in relation to one another and in the complexities of a wider context, including in some instances the radically different mystery of some ultimate transcendent source of all there is, they were exhibiting what is most distinctive and beyond ordinary explication in our awareness of ourselves. This is very strikingly evident in the work of Gabriel Marcel to which I now turn.

Marcel returns repeatedly, in meditative and more impression-istic works, like *Being and Having*, and in more systematic and comprehensive statements of his views, like his two volumes of Gifford Lectures, with the general title *Mystery of Being*, to the themes of mystery and the peculiar way in which the self, at the core of it, is 'uncharacterisable'[27] or 'rebellious to descriptions'.[28] He presents this extensively in terms of an inwardness of ex-perience and a something beyond the Me which has qualities and can be identified in terms of them. 'To identify', he declares, 'is in fact to recognise that something, or someone, has, or has not, such-and-such a character, and, conversely, such-and-such a character is relative to a possible identification'.[29] But this is significant only at the level of 'Having', which means here having predicates — 'I return to the category of having in so far as it is implied in the fact, for a subject, of having (i.e. of carrying with it) predicates'.[30] But 'the question "What am I?" has no equivalent on the level of Having'.[31] As it is also put, but a little more obscurely:

> I must develop what I said about the uncharacterisable. We cannot think of a character without attaching it to a subject by the link expressed by the verb *to belong*. But this supposes a sort of pattern whose nature we must try to make clear. We are here in an order which essentially carries with it the use of the expression 'also'; this character is chosen *among* others. We are not, however, faced with a collection, as phenomenalism would have us believe, there is always the transcendence of the *qui*.[32]

Again

> I am again preoccupied by the question what it means to possess qualities. The word 'also' seems to me only to have meaning in the order of Having. Perhaps recourse to the category of Having for thinking of qualities is an expedient, a makeshift necessary if we are to conceive (or persuade ourselves that we conceive) the juxtaposition of qualities.[33]

But to think of myself in these ways, in the world of Having, as being characterised by qualities or predicates, is also to think of myself in terms of 'disposability'. At a certain level, or in a certain way, we have to think in terms of qualities or predicates, to be 'conscious of being fixed within a zone or determinate scale'.[34] But this is only 'what a superficial inquiry would seem to show',[35] and it is when we think of ourselves as being 'non-disposable' persons that we are liable also to 'self-preoccupation'. We have an 'ego-centric topography' which can only be corrected in 'encounters' which make us 'sharply aware of the accidental character of what I have called our mental space, and of the rigidities on which its possibility rests'.[36]

In these latter nuances we seem to be passing into a somewhat different universe of discourse for the main theme, or a different setting, and it becomes clear that what we are led to is the transcendence of the level of characterisation and determinate qualities. This is what detachment and charity 'as absolute disposability'[37] properly involve. 'The world of the Same and the Other is the world of the identifiable'.[38] But love transcends the opposition of the same to the other by planting us in Being'.[39] This is the proper 'transcendence of the *qui*' already mentioned. It is 'a function of the attitude I take up in the face of the *qui*'.[40]

What sets out therefore as a promising account of 'the distinction between what we have and what we are',[41] in terms of an ultimate identity of the individual person which is not reducible to attributes and history, becomes inflated into the totally different consideration of divine or absolute transcendence. Characterisation belongs to the world of limited, finite, existences and their relations, but God, as infinite being, is, in his essence beyond this, however hard that thought may be. This is why 'any doctrine of the Attributes would tend inevitably to lead us astray. The *I am that I am* of Scripture would be truly the most adequate formula from an ontological point of view'.[42]

This is no doubt important, however much it may admit of being qualified in other ways. It has also a bearing, for those who accept it, on our conspectus on everything else, the world of nature and our personal and moral relations. But it is an entirely different concern. The elusiveness of our own identity is very peculiarly bound up with the finality of the distinctness of persons, their irreducible individuality, and it is in this context, where the other retains its integrity as distinct existence, that love and detachment have their proper place, not in a metaphysical dilution of self and other in an extension of strictly religious transcendence to all there is. The sense in which the self is non-characterisable has a very important place in a final religious view, but in itself it is religiously neutral and can be admitted quite as properly by the agnostic as by the believer. To acknowledge that there is 'a kind of mystery there', though that term is not the most apposite to what is at the core of self-awareness, does not require us to 'believe we could find a whole theory of the Thou within it'.[43] The 'thou' at the finite level is a quite separate issue.

The same themes, presented by Marcel in a loose and somewhat exploratory impressionistic way in *Being and Having*, become the core of the more exhaustive and systematic presentation of his views in his Gifford Lectures, *Mystery of Being*.[44] But the outcome is the same, and what we find in miniature in *Being and Having* is on the whole more perspicuous and easy to apprehend than the suppositions to which we are led through extended deviations in the Gifford Lectures. In Volume 1 of the latter we read much that is suggestive and promising about the 'disquieting ambiguity'[45] of talk about the self and the complications of 'self-discovery' and entering 'into the depths of one's self',[46] and 'the pure immediacy expressed by the "I exist"',[47] and also about the inwardness and mystery of selfhood. The account we might give of ourselves in filling a form for an official is rejected[48] as utterly inadequate, indeed beside the point, in answer to the question 'Who am I, really?'. The answers that I give to satisfy the official, or anything like it that I might just invent, are like shabby garments, not my own, and 'I have to protest: I am not this garment'.[49] Marcel declares:

> The real fact, the thing that complicates the whole business, that is, the truth of it, is that I am myself and not somebody else; if I were somebody else, the question would be put again, when my turn came up, but it would still be exactly the same sort of question. There is thus, or so it seems to me, a sense in which I am not a definite somebody; from the moment when I start to reflect, I am bound to appear to myself as a, as it were, non-somebody linked in a profoundly obscure fashion, with a somebody about whom I am being questioned and about whom I am certainly not free to answer just what I like at the moment when I am being questioned.[50]

We have thus 'a paradox' 'that I appear to myself both as a somebody and not a somebody'.[51] The problem is then to 'get a closer grip on this experience of the self as not being a somebody'.[52] In similar contexts there are references to a 'veiled reality'[53] and the declaration that the 'immediacy of self-awareness is crusted over by habits and by all the superstructures of an official, compartmentalized life'.[54] Between ourselves and existence we are interposing thicker and thicker screens'.[55] There is, we are told, a 'non-transparency' of personal existence.

All this might seem, from my point of view, to be entirely on the right lines. This is why some who share my views are encouraged to find support, as they take it, in the sort of Continental philosophy to which I am referring in this chapter. And, to some extent, they are warranted to do so. The self in its more than characterisable form is brought into prominence. But our allies are in fact more uncertain than they seem. For what lies beyond the screen, in the 'immediacy of self-awareness' and its non-transparency, is not the ultimate individual subject, but, in ways partly reminiscent of what was more explicitly maintained in idealist metaphysics, some extension or completion of the individual into a context where its proper reality is wholly absorbed into its significance in transcendent being — in the strict sense.

This can be seen well in what is said about the words 'my body'. We cannot give an exhaustive account of the body in biological terms. It is the body of some person, my body is mine; and we have to ask, as one of the central questions in philosophy, how the mind is related to the body. What does my ownership of my body involve? Marcel gets to the heart of the problem, as he understands it, with the strange insistence that my body is mine in the same sense in which my dog belongs to me. But even allowing for a sense in which a dog is mine other than legal ownership, the dog is attached to me, obeys me etc., this is far removed from the sort of question we have in asking how my body belongs to me. For Marcel, however, 'my link with my body' is really the model 'to which I relate all kinds of ownership'.[56] But, to sustain this, it must also be held that 'I *am* my body'.[57] I certainly cannot be 'reduced to a completely dematerialized ego'.[58] But to this end we have to think 'of the body not as an object but as a subject'.[59] The body, 'as properly mine' is 'something felt; I am my body only in so far as I am a being that has feelings'.[60] But this again is not to be thought of 'as a sort of kernel of *subjective* certitude'.[61] For we have 'passed beyond the interpretation of sensation as the transmission and reception of a message'.[62] For that requires some 'mediation' and that 'ad infinitum', for we give it a 'determinate spatial locus' in 'the infinite network of determinate spatial loci in general'.[63] We must pass 'beyond the limits of idealism' and 'beyond the interpretation of sensation as the transmission and reception of a message',[64] the main concern here being, it seems, to avoid the menace of solipsism; when I talk of myself as a 'physical apparatus' it is 'not really about *myself* that I am talking'.[65] We have to bring in instead the notion of 'an existential immediate, that is to say, of something I *am*',[66] and this involves 'non-objective participation' illustrated in the notion that when people are praying together they are 'melted into a single love.'[67]

The last supposition is what gives us our key to the complexities of this discussion in which 'I am my body', but not in any ordinary sense. Marcel seems to dissolve any problems we may have about ourselves and our bodies, and ourselves and other persons also, in one insistence on an all-embracing transcendent. The mystery of this is the model of all mysteries, and it is the one thought that is to be invoked to solve all our problems. Even 'the peasant's soil transcends everything he sees around him' and 'is linked to his inner being'.[68] The self is also essentially 'in a situation'. It cannot be stripped of 'the empirical self', for there is an 'ingathering' such that 'the reality, confronting which one ingathers oneself, itself becomes a factor in the ingathering'.[69] This does not imply a doctrine of a 'universal mind'[70] but rather some 'togetherness' 'between the landscape and me' by which I 'transcend the opposition of my inner and outer worlds'[71] and achieve also an 'inter-subjectivity',[72] an 'awareness of a suprapersonal unity'[73] in which persons are subsumed in such a way that 'the words *I* and *You* cease to denote two nuclei quite distinct from each other',[74] telepathy being thought to be inconceivable if we think in those terms.

This is not thought to be 'a mere flat denial of continuing personal identity',[75] for there is 'a continuity of an historical becoming'[76] at some level where we do distinguish between 'He, She or It',[77] but there is also a 'dimension beyond life's probing'[78] — where 'the opposition of the successive, as such, and the abstract, as such, can be transcended at a supratemporal level which is also, as it were, the very depth or inwardness of time',[79] the mystery of 'the absolute Here-and-Now', 'the trans-historic depth' of the Eternal Thou.

Viewed in this way, the mystery, and the essential inwardness and elusiveness of the self, are not indications of something peculiarly characteristic of selfhood and personal identity, but of some all-inclusive union of all things in a mystical monism where all our normal problems simply disappear. By contrast, I have been holding that, however important it may be to recognise the transcendent and the depth it gives to finite existence, we are not unaware of what we are except in the inability to characterise it beyond each one's apprehension of himself in being himself, a mystery, if the term is appropriate at all, which essentially involves and underscores the ultimate distinctness of persons which is much imperilled in the peculiar course of the emphasis on depth and inwardness in the speculations of Gabriel Marcel.

We find very much the same situation, in essentials, in the work of other writers who do not have the explicit religious motivation of Marcel or any proper recognition of a strictly transcendent source of present existence, though they use the term in a rather different way. Conspicuous among these is J. P. Sartre, the outstanding existentialist philosopher. Even more than Marcel his own involvements were many, including the world of general literature as well as academic study. This has made it seem especially impressive to many who welcome this broad concern, and insight into the emphases appropriate at present, that he should have brought questions of personal existence and involvement to the centre of the stage, for himself and others.

A great deal of Sartre's more severely philosophical thinking takes its course as a reaction against the teaching of his own original mentors, especially Husserl and Heidegger, and in particular as the retention in subtle ways, of features of the thought of these thinkers which he seemed to be most firmly rejecting. He never broke away entirely from their spell. This accounts, more I suspect than the particular cast of his own mind and his style of writing, for the difficulty of making his own position precise enough and for the paradoxical character of his central themes. The pre-eminence of consciousness for his own system is clear, and however difficult it may be to discover how precisely this must be understood, it is certain that any form of materialism or of positivism is being rejected. There is some sense, and that of radical importance for Sartre, in which mental existence is genuine and matters; and yet, in the account that he gives of it, it seems to melt away into preconceptions about what the world in general must be like. Insights into states of mind and crucial situations of personal perplexities and decisions tend to be overlaid by permutations of thought which partly ring the bell and partly bewilder.

It would be a very complicated business to follow this out in all its ramifications in Sartre's writings, and as with other thinkers who present us with highly convoluted systems of thought, there is a risk in seeking to lay hold of a few indisputable themes — we may do injustice to other things that are said. But it is a risk worth taking, for the desperation with which Sartre struggles to maintain an accceptable position, in the varieties of his acceptances and repudiations, seems to me to highlight very clearly the need for a view of the self of the kind I am seeking to present in this book.

The main ambiguity is that of the nature of consciousness itself. Sartre makes a move now very familiar when he observes:

> When I run after a streetcar, when I look at the time, when I am absorbed in looking at a portrait, no I is present. There is consciousness of the streetcar having-to-be-caught, etc., and non-positional consciousness of that consciousness. On these occasions I am immersed in the world of objects; they constitute the unity of my consciousness; they present them-selves with values, with qualities that attract or repel — but I have disappeared, I am nothing. There is no place for Me at this level of consciousness. This is not accidental, it is not due to a temporary lapse of attention, but to the structure of con-sciousness itself.[80]

Just how must all this be understood? 'The world of objects' itself constitutes 'the unity of my consciousness'. Could this be interpreted in a severely phenomenalist sense, objects being just objects of consciousness? This would be hard to reconcile with the strong realist streak in Sartre's thought. It is 'the being of the world which is implied by consciousness', 'this table, this package of tobacco'.[81] In opposition to the idealists, Sartre insists that it is the real world that we apprehend, in the appearance themselves, 'not a noumenal being which is hidden behind them'.[82] But is the unity and being of consciousness itself then just some aspect or modification of the world as presented, is this what is meant by 'constitutive consciousness', a consciousness of things which are 'transcendent' in the sense of not being exhaustively presented, but where the consciousness is also 'immanent'? Is there no ultimate wedge to be driven between consciousness and the world apprehended?

One point which Sartre certainly has in mind here is that there is no pure consciousness, in the sense maintained by some mystics — especially in the East — namely a consciousness with no sort of object; consciousness for Sartre must always be 'of' something, and, in this, I for one readily concur. But it does not follow that consciousness is not something to be prised apart from the world it apprehends. The position is made more difficult when Sartre, in line with bolder reductionists, diverts attention to dispositional matters and irrelevances, for the present issue, such as the ability to ask questions. This may be important in some aspects of understanding what consciousness is like, but it does nothing to indicate what it is to be conscious in distinction from the world being there.

This is not eased by talk of 'self-reflective' consciousness, because this itself, as in Ryle's account of being self-conscious, is understood in terms of special ways of noting things and of activity, akin to noting peculiarities of any experience which is mine without considering any more basic sense in which they are mine or belong. But even if we hesitate to take Sartre the whole way with reductionist and immanentist views of consciousness, one thing is clear — he has no place for a proper subject as a distinct existent required to make sense of our being conscious at all. As stated in the quotation above — 'I have disappeared, I am nothing'. There is simply 'the unitary organization of immanence',[83] or as it is also put:

At the limit of coincidence with itself, in fact, the self vanishes to give place to identical being. The self can not be a property of being-in-itself. By nature it is reflexive ... The *self* refers, but it refers precisely to the *subject*. It indicates a relation between the subject and himself, and this relation is precisely a duality, but a particular duality since it requires particular verbal symbols. But on the other hand, the *self* does not designate being either as subject or as predicate . . . In fact the *self* cannot be apprehended as a real existent . . .[84]

Or, as we also read: 'To introduce into the unity of a pre-reflective *cogito* a qualified element external to this *cogito* would be to shatter its unity, to destroy its translucency; there would then be in consciousness something of which it would not be conscious and which would not exist in itself as consciousness'.[85]

This is even more starkly put in another context:

Phenomenology can still be reproached for providing an escapist doctrine, for drawing a piece of man out of the world, and thereby turning our attention away from real problems. It seems to me that this reproach no longer has any justification, if the Me is made an existent strictly contemporaneous with the world, whose existence has the same essential characteristics as the world . . . It is sufficient that the Me be contemporary with the World and that the subject — object dualism, which is purely logical, finally disappear from the preoccupations of philosophers.[86]

Not surprisingly, Professor Peter Caws sums up the position in an excellent concise survey of Sartre's treatment of consciousness and subjectivity[87] when he says: 'The Sartrian Ego has the elusiveness of a burst bubble, and the outcome of the analysis is an empty I, correlative to a Me reduced to nothingness, together maintaining a spontaneous unity of states and actions'.[88]

These tortuous moves and ambiguities are not, however, without significance. I have followed them, in the case of Sartre as of the other philosophers discussed in this chapter, in outline but with as much explicit reference to actual text as reasonable space would allow, because they seem to me, in their persistence and influence as much as in their difficulty and ambiguity, to show what obstacles and frustration we set up for ourselves if we fail to appreciate that, at the core of all awareness, there is the self which *is* aware and which must itself be understood to be an entity, as much as entities in the world around us, but with the peculiarity that it cannot be known or described like external objects in terms of special attributes, but only in the awareness of himself that each one has in his own case in any experience whatsoever. With this allowed, the seeming emptiness and elusiveness of mental existence can be properly appreciated, as they are only dimly recognised in the writings to which I have just been alluding, without desperately seeking to reduce them in turn to external reality or some phenomenological account of what we find our actual experiences to be or to involve. Acknowledge the proper elusiveness of the self and we can be spared much wandering in alluring mazes from which there is no proper exit.

10 The Plus of Determination

The writings of Nicolai Hartmann were highly esteemed in the early part of this century, and very widely read. In many quarters they appear since then to have passed into oblivion, although I was pleased, in making a reference to him, and his relevance to current controversy, at a recent Joint Session of the Mind Association and the Aristotelian Society, to find that more persons than I anticipated were interested in him and convinced of his importance for us today.

The third volume of Hartmann's *Ethics* is peculiarly relevant to the main contentions of this book, and especially so his notion of 'a plus of determination'. This is the idea of some new mode of determination which supervenes upon other processes without suspending them or modifying what they are in themselves or at their own level, and without requiring any gap in the initial course of things into which the new factor may interpose itself. No change is required in the way we understand the original determination, chemistry is chemistry and physics is physics, but processes of that sort could have their part, strictly in terms of what they normally are, in a more comprehensive whole in which the eventual course of things owes much to the supervention of other factors as well as the forces already at work.

It may not be easy to determine how far, if at all, this applies to processes below the level of sentience. It is, indeed, quite common to refer to the functions of some inanimate artefacts, like computers, in some sorts of mentalistic terms. The computer, it is sometimes said, calculates, is puzzled, tells or informs or redirects itself, is surprised, pleased, or even angry. But this is surely no more than a helpful metaphorical way of referring to highly elaborate processes which have some resemblance to conscious operations but which must also be understood, in the final

177

analysis, in terms of the strictly material operations of machines which men have made and whose operations they condition in the process known as 'feeding in information'.

Those who wish to deny that there is more than an analogy here usually do so in the interest of a reductionist or behaviourist view of properly mental processes themselves. If my anger can be described entirely in terms of my observable reaction, then there does not seem to be much impropriety in the characterisation of a machine in literally the same sense. But of all views in the philosophy of mind this appears to me to be the most naive and implausible. However 'clever' the machine may be, it still operates, as a strictly material entity, in ways which the designers of it can exhaustively understand in the terms in which any physical contrivance is known to work.

On themes of this kind, if anything further is needed, it has been said already by me, earlier in this book and elsewhere, and by many others. But the view may still be advanced that in some 'organic' processes, as they are sometimes described, the operations of some units cannot be understood entirely in terms of sub-processes within them considered by themselves or in some summation. The way the processes are related, or the nature of the whole, makes a difference. I find it hard, however, to think of a proper instance of this which would require the recognition of a properly new order of determination.

The case for something of this kind, even at the inorganic or physio-chemical level, has however been very helpfully investigated in the symposium on Cognitive Biology conducted at the Joint Session of the Mind Association and the Aristotelian Society in 1980 by Dr Margaret Boden and Dr Susan Khin Zaw.[1] Dr Boden sets out fairly boldly to maintain that the biologist must go beyond the level of physio-chemical process and strictly molecular biology. 'Even processes whose underlying biochemical details are relatively clear may not be intelligible in terms of molecular biology alone'.[2] There is 'adaptive behaviour' which needs to be 'defined at a higher level than molecular biology'.[3] At the same time this must not be understood in terms of properly 'mentalist implications', in the words used subsequently by Dr Zaw.[4] We are not invited to reinstate some form of vitalism or animism as was current some while ago, or 'an up-dated attribution of a soul',[5] again in Dr Zaw's words. But if there is no subtle form of mentalism, just what is the force of the cognitive terminology?

What happens when we pass beyond the strictly physio-chemical approach?

The kind of example we are offered here is that of oscillations within a biological system, a sort of 'biological clock', which initiate waves of activity which travel over greater distances than in the case of 'gradient fields by way of simple diffusion. This means that they might be able to influence the organism as a whole, rather than just that extent of tissue which is within a diffusible distance'.[6] It is not easy for the layman to decide the precise significance of this, or appreciate how far, if at all, it does take us beyond physio-chemical processes in a full presentation of the story as a whole. But if we are impelled, in cases of this kind, to go beyond molecular biology, not as a provisional move pending a fuller account, but as a final notion of the way things are, we do indeed seem to have an example of a mode of determination which takes up other processes into a unity where determination as a whole is different.

Even so, one hesitates to characterise the total or superior process in cognitive terms. If there is no mental or sentient factor involved, can we understand the cognitive characterisation in any way other than as helpful, fanciful metaphors? That metaphors may be useful in this way need not be denied, and it could well be that, at a certain stage of research, investigation is best directed on the supposition of some quasi-cognitive activity beyond which we cannot go at the time. As a methodological device to get us to the right questions there may be much to be said for a cautious use of cognitive concepts in biology, it might make us more open and adventurous in our mastery of the subject. But that in itself would not imply that we had passed to a totally new conception of the subject.

Dr Boden herself is fairly firm in following Goodwin in his insistence that 'cognitive terminology in describing biological systems is not a fanciful metaphor'.[7] On the other hand it is far removed from conscious reasoning and more akin to 'non-introspectible cognitive structures' which psychologists take to 'underlie conscious thought, experience and behaviour'.[8] There can be an extension of concepts from a primary domain to a secondary one, and this can be useful in directing empirical research. But even so one would take some convincing, in the present instance, that anything significant had been found between some sort of mentalistic process, rightly rejected here, and a provisional metaphorical device which had no ontological significance.

It is to the latter conclusion that Dr Zaw inclines. She hesitates to go all the way with reductionism, but accepts its intuition about the scientific mode of understanding the world, namely that 'physicalism is somehow intrinsic to empirical science as we now conceive it. Physicalism constrains its ontology: the kinds of things there are, in the world of science, are *physical* kinds'.[9] It does not follow that all understanding in science must be in terms of physics and chemistry, but it must 'be in some sense anchored in or constrained by the physical world. Reductionism is an attempt to formulate this anchoring — wrong, as it turned out. But the desire to anchor was sound'.[10]

The point at which Dr Zaw veers a little towards Dr Boden's position, or makes at least a provisional concession to it, is in her reference to functional explanation. This is not itself a physicalist explanation. A football is shaped as it is for kicking, a cap on the distributor to keep it dry. But this goes beyond a proper physical explanation. It refers to the purpose of the designer or maker, and as such it is perfectly legitimate as an explanation of these physical things, but it is quite different from the mechanical explanation. We could explain how a bicycle works without reference to the point of making it. But the latter is legitimate although it 'does not threaten the mechanical explanation of a bicycle'.[11] But does this affect biology? We may, if so disposed, invoke a divine author and sustainer of the external world and ascribe to him various purposes in making it as it is. But that in itself, whatever difference it made to the scientist's general view of his work, hardly enters into what he actually does and maintains as a scientist. The question is whether something of a like functional sort can be found at other levels which are strictly relevant to what the biologist does beyond guiding him, through metaphorical suppositions, to ways of directing his study which he might not otherwise appreciate, but which must eventually be cashed in physical terms.

It is this sort of question that Dr Boden, and those of like mind, have to answer in terms of explicit examples. It is not enough to show that functional explanations cannot as such be reduced to biochemical ones. The question is whether such explanations are in the last analysis necessary at all. 'A physicalist need not deny that it is possible and even useful to regard organisms as information-exchanging devices; the point is that no one would regard such an account as a *scientific* explanation if it did not have a conceivable physical basis or realization'.[12] It is for those who question this to provide persuasive examples.

There is one feature of these issues, however, which seems to have been left out of account altogether by both writers, understandably since it cannot have much, if any, place in the contexts with which they have concerned themselves. I refer to the fact of sensation. The moment we pass to properly animal existence, we must reckon with this. In the case of the higher animals there is much more than mere sensation, co-ordination of vision and perspective, for instance. A dog sees very much as we do, and smells and hears. He chases the ball to the far corner of the garden because he sees it rolling that way, he barks at the stranger because he sees him approaching, he leaps up with excitement when you reach for the lead, he yelps because he feels pain. Indeed the level of intelligence, however sharp its limitations, can be very high as anyone watching a dog penning sheep can see; and, as I have earlier stressed, to give a Rylean or quasi-Rylean behaviourist account of this would be as absurd as it is in our own case. But if this is so, we must take account of it in a total story of animal life, though for many physiological purposes we can disregard it.

Whether sentience comes in, and makes a difference, at the level of biological study with which the two symposiasts were concerned, is another matter. Presumably the embryo does become sentient at some stage well before birth. It clearly does not do so in a way that directly involves the way the body is formed and develops. It must be of a very rudimentary kind. But it might be worth considering in these contexts whether, in some subtle way, the onset of sentience, at whatever stage it comes, makes a difference. If it does, in this or in other respects, then we do have a new feature of determination which affects the course of things without being reducible, at any stage, to biochemical processes.

A similar problem to that discussed by Dr Boden and Dr Zaw could be raised at a lower level of animate existence, in botany. In earlier forms of vitalism much would be made of the way a plant shapes its own life and heals some damage done to it. Would Dr Boden's arguments apply here also, and could they be met in the same terms by Dr Zaw? It would seem, on the face of it, that Dr Boden's approach would be harder to support here, and yet there is at least some initial plausibility in the case, which certainly strikes the layman with much force, that the processes involved in vegetable life are organic and peculiar in a way of which an exhaustively physicalist story could not be told. If that were the case, then there would here also be a form of determination beyond the constitutive processes initially involved.

I should like to interpolate here the further comment that the relevance of the issue, as presented in the symposium, to questions of the conservation of nature and respect for living things, is nil. As Dr Zaw points out, we can get no mileage out of Dr Boden's claims in this way; and that, it seems to me, holds irrespective of the soundness of these claims. We conserve the world of nature mainly because of its importance, for use and enjoyment, by human beings; and we care for animals and their environment because they also enjoy such amenities in their way, and can be hurt by the lack of them. We are kind, and not cruel, to brutes because they *feel* pain. To put this very starkly, and leave out religious considerations that may be relevant, would it really console us at all, on being assured that all life would be extinct on our planet the next day, to be told also that there would still be wooded glades and winding rivers and stormy seas and snowy peaks? In romantic ways we might still deplore the passing of these, but if there is no enjoyment of them, at the very least in rudimentary sentience, would it matter two hoots if the world were burnt to a cinder or became a cloud of gas — apart of course from prospects of renewal. Is it not experience of some sort at least, and the worth that goes with it, that counts in these contexts?

There is no hubris in this. It is not the resemblance to ourselves that matters, but the simple linkage of worth with experience, and if we neglect this, in matters like the conservation of nature, and feel impelled to retreat upon the sort of considerations adduced by Dr Boden, we may find ourselves giving very uncertain hostages to fortune.

I return to Hartmann and the 'plus of determination'. If the views favoured by Dr Boden could be maintained, and their like in other animate existence or, it may be, even in physics and cybernetics, such that the whole story could not be told in principle or eventually in physical terms, then we would have at all these levels clear examples of what Hartmann has in mind. But it does not seem in fact that the case has been made out.

It is quite another matter however once we reach the level of sentience. At rudimentary levels the difference made in practice to response or behaviour may be barely perceptible, but presumably there would be some, notwithstanding the dependence of the sentience on physical conditions. At other levels the difference will be substantial, unless the main contentions of this book are wrong. The dog runs this way rather than that because he sees where the ball goes. The initial significance of Hartmann's concept, for man as for brute, is that in claiming the efficacy of mental states, we do not have to suppose that all other relevant determinations are suspended.

Hartmann himself puts it as follows:

What is contained in the earlier stage (of a causal nexus) necessarily works itself out in the later. Hence the later stage is only in so far determined beforehand by the earlier as no new factors are added. But if such are added, they modify the determinational complex and thereby all the ensuing stages. Herein consists the diversion of the process from its direction. Nothing opposes such a diversion.[13]

That is why an incoming Plus of determination in it is every time simply one component more, which according to its direction and force determines the result.[14]

Precisely this is the peculiarity of the causal nexus, that it does not allow itself to be suspended or broken but does permit of being diverted. The further course of the process then is different from what it would have been if it had lacked the new determinant; but no one of the original causational factors in it is on this account diminished; all are just as efficacious and unhindered in the diverted process as they would have been if no diversion had taken place.[15]

It is in these terms that Hartmann conceives of freedom:

Hence 'freedom' in the positive sense is here actually achieved. It is not a Minus in determination (like 'negative' freedom) but is evidently a Plus. The causal nexus does not admit of a Minus. For its law affirms that a series of effects, once it has entered upon its course, can by no kind of external agency be annulled. It may however very well admit of a Plus — if only there be such

—, for its law does not affirm that no elements otherwise determined could be added to the causal elements of a process.[16]

This allows of many senses of freedom according to the various orders of determination which may be superimposed one upon the other. How many of these there are will depend much on the view we take on issues like the one discussed in the symposium I have just been noting. The modification of physical processes by sentient and experiential or mental factors is one obvious major instance. It is not that the initial causal process is annulled or suspended, but that a further determination combines with it, much as an additional player joining a number of people already propelling a push-ball can make a difference to the way the ball moves. The new player does not have to throw off the persons already there before he can make any impact, neither can he have it all his own way. The nature of the ball itself and other material conditions preclude that. So does the pressure already exerted by other players. But the pressure applied by the new player also makes a difference to what happens.

One form of freedom, in the sense indicated, has much importance. It is that which comes about in the way the various ingredients in our psychological make-up modify one another and bring thus the force of the system of one's nature or character as a whole into the decisions and responses we make and our impact on the world in our conduct. Hegelian and post-Hegelian idealist philosophers made much of this. In appreciating how the abiding subject, as in Kantian philosophy, made possible the apprehension of a unified world of objects, they understood also how the same self, in virtue of holding together our experience as a whole, would bring unity and system to our desiring nature also. In the measure in which this happened in particular cases our aims and aspirations would be considerably modified, the strength of various desires depending much on the 'system of desires' to which they belong. New aims are made possible in the same way. Long-term projects over-ride wishes which might otherwise be much stronger at the time. This is what is usually known as self-determination, and it found a classical expression in Essay 1 of Bradley's *Ethical Studies*.

This kind of self-determination is sharply contrasted with the situation where isolated, or relatively isolated, impulses battle it out in their unmitigated initial strength among themselves, as is presumed to happen for the most part at least among brutes. Although we are, in both cases, dealing with mental as against material determination, there is a considerable difference which warrants the acknowledgment of self-determination, in the sense indicated as a distinct mode of determination. It can therefore claim a place of its own in the stratification of modes of determination envisaged by Hartmann.

This has been thought by many, including foremost idealist writers, to provide the proper solution to the problem of freedom and accountability. Our conduct, in so far as it is self-determined and reflects what we are as rational creatures, is our own and free in the way required by ascription of moral praise and blame. Hartmann would not agree. Psychological determination, in Hartmann's own term, is not enough. But the way the basic problem presents itself to him is in terms of an *aporia* presented especially by Kantian philosophy and the sharpness of the bifurcation into noumenal and phenomenal determination. Against the latter Hartmann presents the view, already outlined, that the causal nexus, while it cannot be suspended, may nevertheless be modified; it is not a world of its own. But he also insists, notwithstanding the firm realism of the axiology defended in the earlier volumes of his *Ethics*, that the apprehension of worth and obligation, although made possible by our rational nature, and indeed described as 'axiological determination', does not of itself guarantee our conformity with them. It is hard, on some aspects of Kantian metaphysics and ethics, to see how the rational self can ever go against its own principles, just as it is hard to see how the hedonistic empirical self can properly heed them. Beyond the axiological determination 'through categories and values', there is a determination 'native to the person himself'.

This determination is not 'without further ado, an actual teleology of values'.[17] 'Of themselves, values have no power to move what actually exists. Such power can only issue from some other quarter, and indeed only from an actual person and in so far as he commits himself to them'.[18] It follows that 'the actual person is autonomous not only when in harmony with the values but also and precisely when opposed to them, that is, that his autonomy as compared with theirs is the higher'.[19] These may not be the terms in which all of us would put these points. But it seems to me that Hartmann is on the firmest possible ground here in recognising a very distinct mode of determination bound up with what it is to be a person.

It is unfortunate, I think, that in his concern to stress the genuineness and distinctness of determination through the agency of a person, Hartmann should also be very averse to describing it as some kind of indeterminism. The reason for this, I suspect, is that he thinks of an undetermined will as a will which wills nothing,[20] blind chance or 'a minus of determination' as he also puts it. But there is in fact a world of difference between chance or sheer randomness and a subject deliberately making a choice between what most appeals to it and what seems to be a duty. This must indeed be the 'positive' decision of the person, but we do not have to suppose that the person is further determined by anything in his nature as a person in this instance beyond what is involved in being a self-conscious person. If there were such a determinant it would have its place in our characters or dispositional natures as a whole, and thus fall into the area of the self-determination noted above.

I think, in the main, that Hartmann would accept this, notwithstanding his insistence that 'all that is ontologically possible is precisely thereby ontologically necessary also'.[21] What he seems really concerned to stand upon is the principle that 'in the real world that only becomes actual for which the total series of conditions is complete'.[22] This is quite compatible with the insistence that one of the conditions, the decisive one, in the case of moral or accountable choice, is the choice made by the agent between genuinely open alternatives.

I will not pursue this theme further here. My reference to the work of Nicolai Hartmann is made, in the first place, for the help it provides in understanding how we can fully recognise the continuing course of physical determination, including processes in the brain, and at the same time recognise the genuine efficacy of mental states. To insist on the latter is in no way an affront to appropriate scientific explanation as such, and I have been much at pains in this book in maintaining that nothing, in the respect we owe to science and empirical study, requires us to suppose that the course of our conduct could be in principle exhaustively accounted for in terms of physical or material determinants.

The second main relevance of Hartmann's views is that they also provide the intellectual framework within which we can properly place and understand the choice which is not itself an expression of our natures or characters, of the sort of persons we are. Many choices are indeed of that kind, they express what we, by our particular constitution, prefer. But this is not bound to be the model for all choice. There supervenes on much that takes its course in one's life, and makes it the kind of existence it is, the exercise of this further peculiar 'plus of determination' which we exhibit in distinctively moral choices and the part these play in due course in our lives and personal relations as a whole.

This is not the place to pursue this particular theme further. There are many ramifications of the notion of the self as a genuine entity not exhaustively described in the peculiarities we ascribe to ourselves as the individuals we are, this elusive essence of selfhood which each one, I have maintained, apprehends initially in his own case. I have outlined more fully what some of these ramifications are, including their place in moral accountability, in the closing chapter of my *The Elusive Mind*, and it would be wasteful to repeat here what I have sketched out already there. My concern in this volume has been to reinforce and extend what was said less completely in my earlier book about the distinctive subject of experience itself and its identity. I hope, in the final volume of this trilogy, to bring out more exhaustively the way the proper understanding of our nature as persons bears on the main concerns we have in morality and religion, and in other aspects of our cultural and social existence.

NOTES

CHAPTER 1 DUALISM RESTATED

1. And in *The Self and Immortality* (Macmillan, 1973), ch. 4.
2. I have used this term, in my paper 'Ultimates and a Way of Looking' first published in *Contemporary Aspects of Philosophy* edited by Gilbert Ryle and reproduced in my *Persons and Life after Death*, to indicate those matters which we seem bound to accept without requiring further reasons.
3. *The Elusive Mind*, chs I-III especially.

CHAPTER 2 SOME RECENT OBJECTIONS TO DUALISM

1. D. M. Armstrong, *A Materialist Theory of Mind* (Routledge & Kegan Paul, 1968) p. 86.
2. Ibid., p. 88.
3. Ibid., p. 88.
4. Ibid., p. 89.
5. Ibid., p. 90.
6. Ibid., p. 89.
7. Ibid., p. 92.
8. Ibid., p. 89.
9. Ibid., p. 90.
10. Ibid., p. 103.
11. Ibid., p. 102.
12. Ibid., p. 93.
13. Ibid., p. 93.
14. Ibid., p. 93.
15. Ibid., pp. 93-4
16. Ibid., p. 94.
17. Ibid., p. 94.
18. Ibid., p. 101.
19. Ibid., p. 101.
20. Ibid., p. 104.
21. Ibid., p. 105.
22. Ibid., p. 105.
23. Ibid., p. 105.
24. Ibid., p. 105.
25. Ibid., p. 105.
26. Ibid., p. 106.
27. Ibid., p. 106.

28. Ibid., p. 107.
29. R. Rorty, 'Incorrigibility as the Mark of the Mental', *The Journal of Philosophy*, 1970.
30. Ibid., p. 414.
31. Ibid., p. 418.
32. Ibid., p. 419.
33. Ibid., p. 420.
34. Ibid., p. 420.
35. Ibid., p. 421.
36. May 1978. This is one of many articles in this journal prompted by a fine paper, 'Is there a Good Argument against the Incorrigibility Thesis?' by Frank Jackson in the same journal for May 1973. The article by Brian Ellis, for example, 'Avowals are More Corrigible than You Think' (*Australasian Journal of Philosophy*, August 1976), centres, like that of Doppelt, on the judgements that we make about our particular experiences. Jackson concentrates on the difficulty of finding a conclusive argument against the incorrigibility thesis. I take a more positive line that it is inherently impossible for a person to be mistaken about what his experience is, even though he may make some mistake in reporting it — and of course in accounting for it.
37. Rorty, op. cit., p. 418.
38. Ibid., p. 418.
39. Ibid., p. 421.
40. Ibid., p. 422.
41. Ibid., pp. 422-3.
42. Ibid., p. 423.
43. J. A. Passmore, *Philosophical Reasoning* (Duckworth, 1970) p. 55.
44. B. Williams, *Descartes: The Projects of Pure Enquiry* (Humanities Press, 1978) p. 292.
45. Ibid., p. 291.
46. Ibid., p. 288.
47. Ibid., p. 289.
48. Ibid., p. 287.
49. Ibid., p. 288.

CHAPTER 3 THE ELUSIVE SELF

1. See his article, 'Self-identity' in *Mind*, 1929, and his *The Modern Predicament*, ch. XVIII (Allen & Unwin, 1955). C.f. also C. A. Campbell, *On Selfhood and Godhood*, chs V–VII (Allen & Unwin, 1957), and A. C. Ewing, *Value and Reality* ch. IV (Allen & Unwin, 1973), and my own *The Self and Immortality*, chs 2 and 3 (Macmillan, 1973).
2. James Ward, *Psychological Principles*, pp. 378-9.
3. Ibid., p. 379.
4. For example in *The Elusive Mind*, ch. XIV and XV.
5. Cf. the chapter 'The Importance of the Body' in my *The Self and Immortality*.
6. In a broadcast discussion reproduced in my *Persons and Life after Death*, ch. 4.

7. See D. Metzler, 'An Essay on H. D. Lewis' Theory of Self-Identity' in *Mind and Nature*, (Department of Philosophy, Emory University) p. 18.

CHAPTER 4 THE SELF AS DESCRIBED – AND MEMORY

1. See, for example, W. D. Ross, *Foundations of Ethics*, ch. VII (Oxford University Press, 1976).
2. Freeman Wills Croft, *The Affair at Little Wokeham*, pp. 131–5 and 232.

CHAPTER 5 CONTINUOUS IDENTITY

1. See W. T. Stace, *Mysticism and Philosophy*, ch. 2 (Lippincott, 1960), pp. 85–123 especially, and my own comment in *The Elusive Mind*, ch. XIV, especially pp. 306–11.
2. At a dinner once I sat next to a person who had little matter for conversation besides his 'out of the body' experiences. He seemed to have no notion of the difficulties some might have about accepting his stories, or making sense of them; and, at the expense of what might seem ungracious behaviour for a guest in his country, I pressed my criticisms rather vigorously, especially on the question of evidence and verification. He assured me he was very active 'out of the body', and I asked if he could, on such an occasion, bring something about which could be seen to be different when he 'returned'. But the most I got was this: on one occasion, when 'out of the body' he was watching 'himself' (presumably his normal embodied self) reading a book and he stepped up and moved the marker from the page, but, he added, the original marker stayed there too. I gave up, and just listened, marvelling at my neighbour's almost total lack of perplexity. At the same time, I would have been very reluctant to say in his case that he was just lying.
3. In my paper 'Public and Private Space', *Proceedings of the Aristotelian Society, 1952–53*, reproduced as an addendum in my *The Elusive Self*, p. 329–42.

CHAPTER 6 IDENTITY AND CONTINUITY OF EXPERIENCE

1. T. Penelhum, *The Philosophy of Parapsychology*, Parapsychology Foundation (New York, 1977) p. 180.
2. D. Parfit, 'Personal Identity', *Philosophical Review*, 1971, p. 11.
3. Ibid., p. 3.
4. Ibid., p. 4.
5. Ibid., p. 6.
6. Ibid., p. 6.
7. Ibid., p. 6.
8. Ibid., p. 6.
9 For further discussion of this point see my *The Self and Immortality*, ch. 6, pp. 106–13.
10. Parfit, op. cit., p. 7.

11. Ibid., p. 8.
12. Ibid., p. 9.
13. Ibid., p. 10.
14. Ibid., p. 11.
15. Ibid., p. 14.
16. Ibid., p. 15.
17. Ibid., p. 15.
18. Ibid., p. 15.
19. Ibid., p. 16.
20. Ibid., p. 16.
21. Ibid., p. 16.
22. It is added here that this 'vindicates the "memory criterion" of personal identity against the charge of circularity' (p. 16). But, as has been pointed out already, there are better ways of doing that.
23. Parfit, op. cit., p. 16.
24. Ibid., p. 17.
25. Ibid., p. 17.
26. Ibid., p. 17.
27. Ibid., p. 17.
28. Ibid., p. 23.
29. A. O. Rorty (ed.), *The Identity of Persons* (University of California Press, 1976) p. 18.
30. Ibid., p. 18.
31. Ibid., p. 20.
32. Ibid., p. 21.
33. Ibid., p. 20.
34. Ibid., p. 21.
35. Ibid., p. 21.
36. Ibid., p. 22.
37. Ibid., p. 22.
38. Ibid., p. 22.
39. Ibid., p. 20.
40. Ibid., p. 23.
41. Ibid., p. 23.
42. Ibid., p. 23.
43. Ibid., p. 23.
44. Ibid., p. 25.
45. Ibid., p. 26.
46. Ibid., p. 27.
47. Ibid., p. 27.
48. Ibid., pp. 27-8.
49. Ibid., p. 28.
50. Ibid., p. 29.
51. Ibid., p. 31.
52. Ibid., p. 31.
53. Ibid., p. 36.
54. Ibid., ch. IV.
55. Parfit, op. cit., p. 95.
56. A. O. Rorty (ed.), op. cit., p. 42.

57. Ibid., p. 43.
58. Ibid., p. 44.
59. Ibid., p. 44.
60. Ibid., p. 45.
61. Ibid., p. 46.
62. Ibid., p. 46.
63. Ibid., p. 46.
64. Ibid., p. 47.
65. Ibid., p. 49.
66. Ibid., pp. 50-1.
67. Ibid., p. 55.
68. Ibid., p. 55.
69. Ibid., p. 56.
70. Ibid., p. 57.
71. Ibid., p. 59.
72. Ibid., p. 59.
73. Ibid., p. 58.
74. Ibid., p. 61.
75. Ibid., p. 73.
76. Ibid., p. 72.
77. Ibid., p. 74.
78. Ibid., p. 74.
79. Ibid., p. 75.
80. Ibid., p. 75.
81. Ibid., p. 75.
82. Ibid., pp. 75-6.
83. Ibid., p. 78.
84. Ibid., pp. 79-80.
85. Ibid., p. 80.
86. Ibid., p. 80.
87. Ibid., p. 80.
88. Ibid., p. 80.
89. Ibid., p. 83.
90. Ibid., p. 83.
91. Ibid., pp. 83-4.
92. Ibid., p. 84.
93. Ibid., p. 84.
94. Ibid., p. 85.
95. Ibid., p. 85.

CHAPTER 7 SOME RELUCTANT CONCESSIONS

1. J. A. Brook, 'Imagination, Possibility and Personal Identity', *American Philosophical Quarterly*, July 1975, p. 187.
2. Ibid., p. 188.
3. Ibid., p. 188.
4. Ibid., p. 188.
5. Ibid., p. 188.

6. Ibid., p. 189.
7. Ibid., p. 189.
8. Ibid., p. 190. Much in the variations on these examples has been prompted by the British Academy Lecture in 1966 by Bernard Williams, entitled *Imagination and the Self*.
9. Ibid., p. 190.
10. Ibid., p. 190.
11. Ibid., p. 190.
12. Ibid., p. 191.
13. Ibid., p. 191.
14. Ibid., p. 191.
15. Ibid., p. 191.
16. Ibid., p. 191.
17. Ibid., p. 192.
18. *The Self and Immortality*, ch. 6.
19. Brook, op. cit., p. 192.
20. Ibid., p. 193.
21. Ibid., p. 196.
22. Ibid., p. 198.
23. Ibid., p. 198.
24. Ibid., p. 198.
25. D. Locke, 'Who I Am', *Philosophical Quarterly*, October 1979, p. 304.
26. Ibid., p. 303.
27. Ibid., p. 304.
28. Ibid., p. 305.
29. Ibid., p. 305.
30. Ibid., p. 309.
31. Ibid., p. 312.
32. Ibid., p. 313.
33. Ibid., p. 314.
34. Ibid., p. 314.
35. Ibid., p. 314.
36. Ibid., p. 314.
37. Ibid., p. 315.
38. Ibid., p. 315.
39. Ibid., p. 316.
40. Ibid., p. 317.
41. Ibid., p. 317.
42. Ibid., p. 318.
43. Ibid., p. 304.
44. In my *Persons and Life after Death* I have discussed critically the view that my 'resurrection body' would be the present body gloriously transformed etc. See pp. 78-87.
45. J. Foster, 'In Self-Defence' in G. F. Macdonald (ed.), *Perception and Identity* (Macmillan 1979) p. 162.
46. Ibid., p. 162.
47. Ibid., p. 162.
48. Ibid., p. 162.
49. Ibid., p. 163.

50. Ibid., p. 163.
51. Ibid., p. 165.
52. Ibid., p. 164.
53. Ibid., p. 164.
54. Ibid., p. 165.
55. Ibid., p. 162.
56. Ibid., p. 172.
57. Ibid., p. 172.
58. Ibid., p. 172.
59. Ibid., p. 173.
60. Ibid., p. 173.
61. Ibid., p. 173.
62. Ibid., p. 174.
63. Ibid., p. 174.
64. Ibid., p. 175.
65. Ibid., p. 176.
66. Ibid., p. 177.
67. Ibid., p. 176.
68. Ibid., p. 177.
69. Ibid., p. 179.
70. Ibid., p. 181.
71. Ibid., p. 181.
72. Ibid., p. 183.
73. Ibid., p. 183.
74. Ibid., p. 183.

CHAPTER 8 SHIFTS OF EMPHASIS

1. R. Wollheim, 'Memory, Experiential Memory and Personal Identity', in *Perception and Identity* (Macmillan, 1979) p. 232.
2. Ibid., p. 210.
3. Ibid., p. 202.
4. Ibid., p. 206.
5. Ibid., p. 206.
6. Ibid., p. 208.
7. Ibid., p. 208.
8. Ibid., p. 208.
9. Ibid., p. 208.
10. Ibid., p. 209.
11. Ibid., p. 209.
12. Ibid., p. 211.
13. Ibid., p. 212.
14. Ibid., p. 213.
15. Ibid., p. 219.
16. Ibid., p. 222.
17. Ibid., p. 223.
18. Ibid., p. 224.
19. Ibid., p. 229.
20. J.R. Jones, *Proceedings of the Aristotelian Society*, Supplement vol. XLI, p. 2.

21. Ibid., p. 16.
22. Ibid., p. 15.
23. Ibid., p. 3.
24. Ibid., p. 3.
25. Ibid., p. 7.
26. Ibid., p. 7.
27. Ibid., p. 10.
28. Ibid., p. 17.
29. Ibid., p. 5.
30. Ibid., p. 6.
31. Ibid., p. 7.
32. Ibid., p. 8.
33. Ibid., p. 9.
34. Ibid., p. 10.
35. Ibid., p. 10.
36. Ibid., p. 11.
37. Ibid., p. 15.

CHAPTER 9 SOME RECENT CONTINENTAL THINKERS

1. Wilhelm Dilthey, *Descriptive Psychology and Historical Understanding*, trans. R. M. Zaner and K. L. Heiges (Martinus Nijhoff, 1977) p. 28.
2. Ibid., p. 28.
3. Ibid., p. 28.
4. Ibid., p. 35.
5. Ibid., p. 29.
6. Ibid., p. 5.
7. Ibid., p. 7.
8. Ibid., p. 31.
9. Ibid., p. 27.
10. Ibid., p. 27.
11. Ibid., p. 27.
12. Ibid., p. 29.
13. Ibid., p. 32.
14. Ibid., p. 32.
15. Ibid., p. 35.
16. H. A. Hodges, *The Philosophy of Wilhelm Dilthey* (Routledge & Kegan Paul, 1952), p. 123.
17. Ibid., p. 125.
18. Ibid., p. 126.
19. Wilhelm Dilthey, *Descriptive Psychology and Historical Understanding*, p. 30.
20. R. A. Makkreel, 'Introduction', in Dilthey, *Descriptive Psychology and Historical Understanding*.
21. *Descriptive Psychology and Historical Understanding*, p. 11.
22. Ibid., p. 10.
23. H. A. Hodges, op. cit., p. 268.
24. R. A. Makkreel, *Dilthey: Philosopher of the Human Studies*, pp. 312–13.

25. Ibid., p. 313.
26. Ibid., p. 313.
27. G. Marcel, *Being and Having*, trans. Katherine Furrer (Dacre Press, 1949) p. 170.
28. Ibid., p. 170.
29. Ibid., p. 153.
30. Ibid., p. 149.
31. Ibid., p. 153.
32. Ibid., pp. 152–3.
33. Ibid., pp. 146–7.
34. Ibid., p. 73.
35. Ibid., p. 73.
36. Ibid., p. 71.
37. Ibid., p. 69.
38. Ibid., p. 153.
39. Ibid., p. 152.
40. Ibid., p. 153.
41. Ibid., p. 155.
42. Ibid., p. 147.
43. Ibid., p. 72.
44. This is the title of two volumes which bear respectively the sub-titles *Reflection and Mystery* and *Faith and Reality*.
45. G. Marcel, *Mystery of Being*, vol. 1, p. 103. I quote here and elsewhere from the Gateway Edition, Chicago.
46. Ibid., p. 162.
47. Ibid., p. 111.
48. Ibid., p. 105.
49. Ibid., p. 104.
50. Ibid., pp. 105–6.
51. Ibid., p. 106.
52. Ibid., p. 107.
53. Ibid., p. 108.
54. Ibid., p. 112.
55. Ibid., p. 112.
56. Ibid., p. 119.
57. Ibid., p. 123.
58. Ibid., p. 120.
59. Ibid., p. 124.
60. Ibid., p. 125.
61. Ibid., p. 135.
62. Ibid., p. 135.
63. Ibid., p. 134.
64. Ibid., p. 135.
65. Ibid., pp. 136–7.
66. Ibid., p. 137.
67. Ibid., p. 140.
68. Ibid., p. 144.
69. Ibid., p. 156.
70. Ibid., p. 107.

71. Ibid., p. 158.
72. Ibid., p. 224.
73. Ibid., p. 223.
74. Ibid., p. 224.
75. Ibid., p. 228.
76. Ibid., p. 230.
77. Ibid., p. 230.
78. Ibid., p. 236.
79. Ibid., p. 239.
80. J. P. Sartre, *Transcendence of the Ego*. I have quoted from the selections, *The Philosophy of Jean Paul Sartre*, edited by Robert Denoon Cumming, pp. 53-4. There is a full translation of *The Transcendence of the Ego* by Forrest Williams and Robert Kirkpatrick (Octagon Books, 1972). The passage I have quoted is found there on pp. 48-9.
81. J. P. Sartre, *Being and Nothingness*, trans. Hazel Barnes, Methuen, 1957, p. LXII.
82. Ibid., p. LXII.
83. Ibid., p. 76.
84. Ibid., p. 76.
85. Ibid., p. 77.
86. *Transcendence of the Ego; the Philosophy of Jean Paul Sartre*, R. D. Cumming (ed.), p. 57; cf. Williams and Kirkpatrick, op. cit. p. 105.
87. P. Caws, *Sartre*, Routledge and Kegan Paul, ch. IV.
88. Ibid., p. 58.

CHAPTER 10 THE PLUS OF DETERMINATION

1. *Proceedings of the Aristotelian Society*, Supplementary vol. LIV, 1980, pp. 25-71.
2. Ibid., p. 27.
3. Ibid., p. 29.
4. Ibid., p. 59.
5. Ibid., p. 69.
6. Ibid., p. 31.
7. Ibid., p. 42.
8. Ibid., p. 41.
9. Ibid., p. 52.
10. Ibid., p. 52.
11. Ibid., p. 58.
12. Ibid., p. 61.
13. N. Hartmann, *Ethics*, vol. III, trans. Stanton Coit, (Allen & Unwin, 1932) p. 69.
14. Ibid., p. 71.
15. Ibid., pp. 55-6.
16. Ibid., p. 55.
17. Ibid., p. 210.
18. Ibid., p. 211.
19. Ibid., p. 193.

20. Ibid., pp. 220-6.
21. Ibid., p. 66.
22. N. Hartmann, *Ethnics*, vol. 1, p. 305.

Name Index

Subject Index